# Am I in Trouble?

## USING DISCIPLINE TO TEACH
## YOUNG CHILDREN RESPONSIBILITY

Richard L. Curwin, EdD
Allen N. Mendler, PhD

*Suggestions for parents, teachers and other care providers
of children to age 10*

Network Publications, a division of ETR Associates
Santa Cruz, CA
1990

© 1990 by Network Publications, a division of ETR Associates. All rights reserved. Published by Network Publications, P.O. Box 1830, Santa Cruz, CA 95061-1830.

10 9 8 7 6 5 4

Printed in the United States of America

Illustrations by Marcia Quackenbush

**Library of Congress Cataloging-in-Publication Data**

Curwin, Richard L.
    Am I in trouble?: using discipline to teach young children re-
sponsibility / Richard L. Curwin, Allen N. Mendler.
      p.  cm.
    "Suggestions for teachers, parents and other care providers of children to age 10."
    Includes bibliographical references.
    ISBN 1-56071-026-8
    1. Discipline of children—United States 2. Communication in the family—United States 3. Parent and child—United States. 4. Responsibility. I. Mendler, Allen N. II. Title.
    HQ770.4.C87  1990
    649'.64—dc20               90-6560
                                   CIP

Title No. 507

*For Sally*

–RC


*For my mother, Ida Mendler, my in-laws, Nancy
and Bernie Klein, and my wife, Barbara, who
model the importance of making their children
the most precious of all gifts; and for my three
children, Jason, Brian and Lisa, who provide
the many joys and challenges that parenting
brings.* –AM

# Contents

# Editor's Preface

This book was written for caring adults as they deal with the challenge of helping children become the best they can be. It is about adult-child relationships—those essential and sensitive interactions that help mold and guide young children. While parents, teachers and caregivers have different roles in the lives of children, they share an important goal—to foster responsible behavior in children.

This book can help those caring adults understand each other's role and perspective. Children don't learn about discipline and responsibility in a vacuum. They learn these lessons from the important adults in their lives—at home, in the classroom, at daycare. They learn about responsibility as they observe adults act responsibly; they learn about respect as they are respected by adults. They learn about dignity as they watch adults treat others with dignity and are themselves treated with dignity by adults.

Because the family provides the essential foundation for a child's view of the world, some sections in the book have more emphasis on family situations and the parents' role. The way life situations impact a child's development will be insightful for teachers and caregivers. Many of the techniques suggested for parents can be easily adapted for use in classroom or daycare settings.

Throughout the book, the authors have offered examples of their suggestions for both teachers and parents. Their examples come from the many, many years they have spent working with children, teachers and other caring adults. Some examples come from their personal experiences as parents and educators. The authors speak to you, the reader, as a friend and colleague—as a caring adult who can have a significant and positive influence on a child.

Kathleen Middleton, MS, CHES
Editor

# Acknowledgments

As with all major projects, there are many people who assisted us both directly and indirectly.

From Al: special thanks are given to my wife, Barbara Mendler, who took over many of the parenting responsibilities, including the primary care of our infant daughter, which freed me to write.

From Rick: special thanks to David, Andrew and Danny Curwin and Leah Blake for teaching me how to parent.

Frank Pasanello, Sue Pratt and Marilyn Roeschle of United Cerebral Palsy of Rochester along with staff at children's and residence program have been so supportive. Thanks also to Patty Fedele, Kay Joslyn, Jeanette Marchant and staff at Webster High School; Paul Scott, Gloria Forgione and staff at Mary Cariola Children's Center; Moe Bickweat, Pete Finch and staff at Oatka Residential Center.

We are especially grateful to Dr. Phil Harris at Phi Delta Kappa, whose support and encouragement of our work is most gratifying. Special thanks also to Dr. Ralph Kester, Betty Osta, Pat Bourcy, Merle Hanley, Georgia Archibald, Sue and Bruce Smith, Dr. Jake Clockedile, Wanda Lincoln, Sam Howe, Dr. Raymond Wlodkowski, Patty Simons, Michael Charles, Meredith Noble, Steve Sanborn and John Namkung and many others, whose appreciation for our *Discipline with Dignity* book provided needed inspiration to write this one.

Finally, Kathleen Middleton, Netha Thacker and staff at ETR Associates/Network Publications have been extraordinary in their competence and unwavering encouragement.

# Introduction

Discipline doesn't start when a child breaks a rule. It starts with a smile, with a hug or when we tuck a child into bed. It starts when we act silly together or share a special song. It starts when we help a child learn to walk and talk and read. Discipline starts with love.

Discipline is typically perceived as negative. The word conjures up images of a child who is bad and parents or teachers who have to straighten the child out. It's as if the child is broken and someone has to fix him or her.

We offer a different picture. As a child develops and learns how to understand and to get along in the world, discipline provides an additional opportunity to learn.

We do not think of children as broken. They don't need fixing. We think of rule violations as a consequence of poor choices. These choices can be improved with increased skill in decision making and greater awareness of the relationship between what children do and what happens when they do it.

A farmer doesn't lecture or scold crops into growing. The farmer provides nutrients, the best topsoil and water to establish the best possible growing environment. In the same way, parents, teachers and caregivers are most effective in discipline when they provide the best possible growing environment.

The underlying theme of this book is that children must learn to be responsible if they are going to survive in our world. The concept of *responsibility* will be discussed in great depth throughout the book. Learning responsible behavior requires that the child's basic needs are met.

Children who are lonely or feel unloved, for example, often choose the easiest way to get attention, even if the outcome is negative. We believe that difficult situations can be minimized or reduced when a child's basic needs are met. The various techniques and methods we suggest have a high probability for success. They emphasize the general value of responsibility and the general goal of meeting the child's basic needs.

Discipline does not exist in isolation. The way we relate to children in play, in times of sadness or in times of sharing is very much related to the way we discipline. This is true for our own children as well as the children we teach and tend.

Discipline is part of the process of learning. It works best when it is an integral part of the total package of parenting and educating children. We believe that the biggest influences derive from many little daily events, not only the major events.

Our view of discipline is to give children the support, encouragement and problem-solving skills they need to fulfill their dreams. When discipline is viewed as a teaching opportunity rather than as a repair, much of the stress of helping children grow and learn is reduced. Many of the battles are minimized, because our challenge isn't to win or to change the child. Our focus is to help the child become better at being who he or she is.

We believe the general goals discussed in this book are universal for anyone who is raising, educating and caring for children. We suggest you treat each example as a possibility rather than a reality. Fill in the mental pictures that depict your own situations. Some individual suggestions might not feel comfortable for you. You may either think of them as experiments and give them a try, or simply ignore those that do not fit in with who you are.

Nurturing children effectively involves the use of a variety of skills based on sound values and attitudes. In a sense, skills are tools which assist us in reaching our goals. Without clearly defined attitudes and values, we cannot apply skills with understanding and continuity.

Even the best skills are not enough without a framework, just as clear, positive attitudes are incomplete without a set of procedures for implementation. What we have consistently tried to avoid is a set of formulas and recipes, which at best provide things to do without considering the context in which incidents occur.

In co-authoring this book, we were faced with a tricky writing problem because there are two of us. We wanted to provide personal examples without constantly saying this is Al talking or this is Rick talking. We solved the problem by simply saying "I" without identifying which of us is the speaker. This greatly simplified the writing without sacrificing the personal nature of the book.

Educating and parenting can be joyous. Discipline can be a joyous task, too. We aren't so idealistic as to think that when children break rules, it's time to celebrate. We aren't naive enough to believe that the serious problems that children face are fun to deal with.

We are naive and idealistic enough to believe that true joy comes from working through difficult times as well as good ones. We believe that as long as we allow children to be themselves, there is always hope—even when things get tough. We hope that the ideas in this book will help you share our idealism.

_____ *Am I in Trouble?*

# Chapter 1

# What Is Discipline?

The challenge of living, loving and working with children is different for each of us. Every child is unique, as is every caring adult. Therefore, each adult-child relationship will have its own challenges and rewards.

Discipline puts structure around relationships. It clarifies the expectations of both children and adults in all kinds of situations. Dignified discipline empowers children and adults, because it establishes guidelines for behavior that respects the rights of both.

As parents and educators, we must first ask ourselves how we want children to behave. We must then ask no less than that from ourselves.

To assess the effectiveness or appropriateness of a discipline method, ask yourself how you would feel if you were at the receiving end of that method. Would it work? Would it change your behavior? Would your dignity be preserved? Would your self-esteem remain intact?

Discipline helps us teach children how to get along effectively with others, what is right, and how to do right. Children do not learn these skills automatically. Just as learning to use a fork, ride a bike or read a book requires skill and practice, so too does learning effective, appropriate behavior for varied situations.

As parents and educators, we sometimes assume that a child will know how to act in a variety of situations. When the child does not act in the manner we thought appropriate, we get angry. We may begin to scold, ignore, lecture, take away privileges or spank.

Children then learn to expect discipline as a negative response to their behavior. They learn that discipline really means punishment.

Relationships with children can test anyone's patience. Yet, it is essential that parents, teachers and other caregivers resist the temptation to speak or act in ways that damage children's self-esteem.

## What Children Need from Caring Adults

Children come to see themselves as special and important when somebody really important wants to be with them, to listen to them, to understand them. The children most likely to develop a positive self-image are those whose parents or teachers or other important people actively look for opportunities to give them what they need.

***Children need to be loved and accepted for who they are.*** Children need to know that they are loved and accepted for the people they are. Acceptance frees children to explore and experiment with new things, things they may be less good at.

Within the safety of the family or with a loving teacher, a child who has difficulty reading may risk the embarrassment of trying a different way. When children know they are cared about simply because they exist, they become more willing to expand outwardly and to attempt that which is difficult.

Most parents quickly recognize that each of their children is different. All teachers know they will have a variety of children in their classrooms. Some children come from affluent families, others from impoverished homes. Some children will come to school already reading, while others will not yet know the alphabet.

During the early preschool and school years, the system has a responsibility to accommodate and accept each child. This is true whether the system consists of parents, educators, scout leaders or others.

Teachers need to learn ways to address children's varying learning styles and needs. To fail to do so, to concentrate instead on children's disabilities or weaknesses, is to set the stage for the development of poor self-esteem, high stress and discipline problems.

Too often, we attach negative labels to children who are different in some way from the norm. We then seek to remediate or fix these children so they are more like everyone else. This can be extremely damaging to a child's sense of well-being.

Labels like attention deficit disorder, hyperactive, learning disabled, behavioral disorder, developmental learning disorder are now a standard part of our lexicon. We tend to place children in special education classes to try to make them learn as other kids do.

And yet, we have frequently observed such children to be very bright, often creative individuals. They may be able to tell great stories, build innovative things, draw with much artistic skill, pull engines apart and put them together again.

We have seen many children with attention deficit disorder sit for long periods of time engrossed in a favorite television show, reading a favorite book or otherwise involved in an activity that requires extensive attention and concentration.

The fact is that we need to send children messages about what they can do, not what they cannot do. We need to focus our primary attention on children's strengths, not their weaknesses. Children will generally live up or down to the expectations that important others have of them.

*Children need you to like yourself.* As parents, teachers and caregivers we are, first and foremost, people with needs that must be met so we can feel satisfied. The extent to which we are able to meet our own basic needs determines how well we are able to provide the support and care that kids need. Parents and teachers who like themselves have more patience and understanding to give children.

Begin by recognizing the good in you. Compliment yourself several times a day. Give yourself a good deal of encouragement. Talk to yourself often. Say things like way to go, I did it, attaboy! Keep a notebook of compliments and self-appreciations, so you can look back on these when you get down.

Unfortunately, we tend to repeat with children the mistakes our parents made with us. It is essential that when those mistakes are especially hurtful, you take care of the healing work you need to do, so you are able to give the children you care for the love and affection they need from you.

*Children need parents and caregivers who can have fun and who give themselves some special time.* If you are feeling satisfied with your life, then you will be much more relaxed and giving with children in a way that will promote healthy growth. Have fun with kids. Norman Cousins found that ten seconds of belly laughter provides the cardiovascular equivalent of ten minutes of intense rowing. Give yourself some special time to do what you want.

*Children need parents and caregivers who manage their stress in productive, appropriate ways.* Parents, teachers and caregivers need to find good ways to unwind, so they have energy to give to children. Increasing numbers of adults are struggling to cope with the many demands of contemporary society. When you learn to manage your stress, you are better able to help children manage theirs.

Both children and caregivers need to learn to identify what stress is, how it can be prevented and how best to manage it. Symptoms of stress include headaches, backaches, feeling irritable, having trouble sleeping or eating, crying, getting into arguments or fights, doing poorly at school and seeking relief through drugs.

Solutions fall into four categories: (1) developing high self-esteem; (2) solving problems that have a solution; (3) learning to keep calm when you don't have the power to solve problems, so they don't keep eating away at you; (4) getting along effectively with other people.

Books such as *Smiling at Yourself: Educating Young Children About Stress and Self-Esteem* (Mendler, 1990) offer many suggestions for parents, educators and caregivers to help children appreciate their own achievements, feel good about themselves and even reward themselves after a job well done.

*Children need to see parents and caregivers working toward realistic, achievable goals.* We are convinced of the importance of modeling or being a living example for children to copy. One of the biggest problems in our society is that there are too few pure heroes left for children to emulate.

Be a hero for children. Let them see you working toward achieving something that is difficult for you—something that requires effort and

e. Let them see how you solve your problems, so they will have a example to follow.

When you have succeeded in achieving your goal or solving your problem, let children see you reward yourself. Let them hear you compliment yourself. Let them see you treat yourself to a well-earned reward for having made it.

In short, let children see that it is admirable to have goals. Let children see that although goals are not always easily attainable, they can be achieved. Show children that rewards should follow the kind of sustained effort that is often required to get ahead in this life.

## Meeting Children's Basic Needs

William Glasser, a well-respected psychiatrist and author, notes that behavior problems result from children's frustration when their basic needs are not met (1984). He teaches us that all people have needs for survival, love and belonging, freedom, fun and power. We add to this list security and competence. Let us look at each of these needs in more detail for an understanding of the need and how we can meet it.

*Survival.* Each human being needs proper physical nourishment in the form of adequate food and drink. Obviously, without adequate provision of either of these, we die. Less obvious, but at least as important, is our need to be touched, held and physically stroked.

Well-known studies have consistently found that without adequate handling, babies and young children appear listless and lose weight and physical conditioning. If severely deprived, these children can become very sick and even die.

To insure that survival needs are being adequately met, offer lots of love in the form of physical handling, holding, gentle touching, hugging and kissing. Displays of these forms of affection are needed throughout a child's development.

It is not possible to spoil children through frequent displays of affection, attention and appreciation. It is, rather, the frequent giving of material rewards that leads to spoiling.

***Love and belonging.*** We all need to feel cared about and connected with others. Children need at least one other person in their lives who thinks they are terrific. They need to feel connected to something larger than themselves, such as a family, club or school group.

When children feel disconnected, they are more likely to either withdraw into themselves or act out in angry, difficult ways to express their loneliness and disappointment. Kids get the important message of belonging when we spend time with them, set appropriate limits and ask them to express feelings, thoughts and opinions.

***Freedom.*** As parents, teachers and caregivers, we must realize there are certain ages and stages that children go through in which they break rules, act out, say no and are otherwise especially challenging. Children behave this way to define themselves as separate from their parent(s).

Misbehavior can be a child's best attempt at establishing her- or himself as a person who is capable of independent thought and action. We are most familiar with adolescence as a peak period of rebelliousness, in which youngsters attempt to define their own independence by challenging the rules and values of their parents. But the normal drive for identity actually begins much earlier.

*Terrible twos, out-of-bounds fours, moody sixes* are a few terms used to describe stages of development in which children's need for freedom may lead to more frequent breaking of rules. Children test limits as a way to learn more about themselves and others.

Effective discipline really means knowing about these ages and stages and combining methods of kindness with firmness to communicate respect for the child's natural thrust towards independence. We recommend Ilg and Ames' *Child Behavior* (1972) for a thorough description of the ages and stages children go through.

***Fun.*** People may be unique in their need for fun. Video games and amusement parks are multimillion-dollar-a-year industries that capitalize on people's need for fun. Children often break rules because it is fun to do so.

Think back to your own childhood. Recall some of the times you broke rules that your parents had for you. Do you remember getting caught for breaking a rule? Even though you may have been punished, can you remember thinking it was worth it?

Chances are pretty good that if you had fun breaking the rule, you might have thought it was worth it even though you were punished. And probably, if you had fun and at the same time were with a friend or two, it was even more exciting and worth the punishment. Why?

Because you were meeting at least two basic needs: fun and belonging. Caregivers need to have fun with children. Find time to laugh with children. When mistakes are made, can you see the light side? It sometimes helps to look at what seems a silly, even annoying thing today, and ask yourself how important the issue will be five years from now.

***Power.*** Children, like adults, need to feel that they can influence people and events around them. Good discipline means helping kids recognize that there are limits and rules that will be enforced by you, the parent, teacher or caregiver. At the same time, children need to feel and believe that their opinions and their points of view are important and will be heard.

In our society, all people who are in positions of authority, including parents and teachers, can no longer simply count on a philosophy of do it my way because I'm older and wiser and I know best. We, like all others in authority positions, must earn the respect of children in order to become meaningful, positive influences.

Naturally, we can force our will on small people. But to do so is to pay the price in resentment, which usually appears later as rebellion and retaliation. We can learn to involve children as good decision makers by giving them some authority to develop rules and consequences that they will live by at home or at school.

Encourage children to volunteer their time and efforts to help other children, senior citizens or the disabled. Children feel very important and special when they can help others.

We want children to develop an internal locus of control, which is associated with positive self-esteem. Look for opportunities for children to be in control of the events around them. These kinds of activities provide healthy ways for kids to feel powerful.

Children also gain a positive sense of power when we are polite to them. We should say please and thank you to children. If we break a promise, we should apologize. These actions speak to children's feelings of self-esteem. Kids who feel good about themselves are less likely to act up in attempts to feel special and important.

*Security.* Children need their lives to be as predictable as possible. With the current high divorce rate in the United States, many children will experience divorce, the remarriage of one or both of their parents, and possibly, living in a blended family or with a stepparent. Any or all of these events create major changes for children and threaten their sense of security.

It is quite normal for children of divorced parents to do much, both in fantasy and reality, to try to reunite their parents. They will do so even when abuse, neglect or major friction was a frequent, if not daily, occurrence in their lives.

Because the need for security is so strong, children need continual reassurance and comfort when traumatic events occur. It is best to be honest with children. Let them know where they will be living and how often they will see the noncustodial parent. Perhaps most important, reassure children that nothing they did caused the divorce.

*Competence.* Children who grow up with healthy self-esteem are able to identify at least one or more areas in which they view themselves as competent. The area of competence may relate to school, athletics, music, community service or a job at home. A frequent suggestion in this book is to catch a child being good.

Kids who become discipline problems are often troubled by low self-esteem. This is often tied to their belief that they aren't good enough. As parents and teachers, our attention needs to be focused most often on effort and personal attainment, rather than comparative achievement with other children. Instead of asking, "What grade did you get?" emphasize "What did you learn?" Share your pride in the accomplishment before you explore ways in which the achievement may be further enhanced.

As professionals and parents ourselves, we are trying and sometimes struggling to raise healthy children amidst a plethora of drugs, violence and poor social role models. We know all kids need to have some important person who cares enough to hug, love, listen and affirm. We know that as a reader of this book, you will want to be that person.

There are many things we can do to minimize the likelihood that children will act out to express their basic needs. All kids will break rules sometimes. Breaking rules is often a healthy expression of the increasing need for independence. Children who see themselves as important, capable, powerful and loved will not need to resort to severe acting-out behavior in efforts to satisfy their basic needs.

Let yourself touch, hold and adore your child. Delight in his or her accomplishments, even if they aren't as good as the neighbor's child. Catch a child being good and appreciate his or her efforts.

When you have lost your temper and said or done something to a child that you know is wrong, apologize. Say please and thank you, and otherwise be as polite as you would be with an acquaintance or even a stranger. Adequate social and emotional nourishment begins at home with you, the parent, the key provider.

If you are a teacher, make each and every child that you touch feel special. Children will remember you far longer than they will remember the content they learned from you.

# Chapter 2

# What Are Rules For?

Use your "inside" voice in the classroom.

Brush your teeth.

Say "no" to rides with strangers.

Treat others nicely.

Look both ways before crossing the street.

Eat your vegetables.

Wear a helmet when you ride your bike.

Bedtime by 8:00 on school nights

Pick up your clothes.

Ask permission to use other people's things

Good discipline requires that parents and teachers learn both to establish rules and to enforce those rules humanely and effectively. Children need to know what is expected of them and what will happen when they act in different ways.

The following conditions are necessary to good discipline:

- Tell children what the rules are.

- Explain why it is important to have rules as soon as children are mature enough to understand.

- Provide clear and firm limits when a rule is broken.

- Develop with the child a plan of action that will assist the child to avoid breaking the rule in the future.

## The Importance of Clear Limits

We often avoid establishing rules because we don't want children to be unhappy. We fear that if we make children cry or feel frustrated, they won't love us. In actuality, nothing could be further from the truth. Children respect and appreciate those who care enough to teach them proper behavior, even if they aren't always happy learning it.

Without limits, the adorable 15-month-old toddler who sits in her or his highchair smearing food on her- or himself or throwing food on the floor could become a six-year-old child throwing food in the school cafeteria. Even at 15 months, a child needs to hear that food is not for throwing.

—A BEDTIME STORY—

Mother wants to put out the light and say good-night to her two-and-a-half-year-old son, Gary, who begins to whine for one more story. At first, Mother is firm. She reminds Gary that this is the last story for the night. Gary, feeling upset and perhaps frustrated, escalates from a whine to a quivering chin that heralds the arrival of a soon-to-be cry.

How could I be such a heartless mother and make my adorable child unhappy? thinks Mother. A caring parent wouldn't make a child cry.

She backs away from the limit and agrees to read Gary the story. Gary learns that whining, crying and feeling unhappy work. He stores these behaviors away in his piggy bank of strategies to use next time he wants something.

We have seen many well-meaning parents, teachers and caregivers give a lot of attention to children when they misbehave. In the process, these adults reinforce or strengthen annoying, difficult behaviors. Let children know with words, body language and your actions that certain rules are important.

This teaches the importance of coping with social demands. Without the opportunity to develop and practice coping skills at home, children may arrive at school, on the playground, in church or in the supermarket without the skills they need to be successful.

It is difficult for many parents and teachers to decide what rules or limits children really need. And in reality, there are no easy answers, especially in the area of minor behaviors.

For example, some parents (or teachers) would say it is important that children keep their rooms (or desks) neat and tidy according to the standards of the parents (or teachers). Others might say that children's rooms or desks belong to them and that it is the children's business to decide how to care for their space.

Others would be somewhere in the middle. They might think that sometimes it is okay for children to decide how their space should look, but at other times (company is coming or the school is holding an open house), the decision is best made by the parent or teacher. These reasonable but different views could and should lead to different rules concerning neatness.

It is neither possible nor desirable for every parent or teacher to establish the same rules for all children. The exact limits or rules depend on our own preferences, children's temperaments, cultural values and attitudes, influences of family and peers. And it is indeed quite challenging for each parent or teacher to decide what is most important.

There is, paradoxically, little conflict among parents and teachers when children act in potentially dangerous or life-threatening ways. All caring and responsible adults agree that children need rules or limits about playing with matches or fire, running in the street, hitting a helpless baby.

We don't worry about a child's frustration or momentary unhappiness at hearing a sharp no when life is endangered. But outside the definite, absolute safety rules, there are often differences of opinion as to when, what, how and where children need to mind.

In addition, children vary greatly in their capacity to learn and follow rules. Some children learn quickly and are readily adaptable. Others may learn slowly or may have a more challenging temperament, so that each rule is greeted with initial defiance.

Some recent studies have found that children's temperaments are more fixed than formerly believed. Particularly at the extreme ends of the continuum, children who are very easy or very difficult to deal with are likely to remain that way for years.

## Destructive Messages

Whatever rules and limits we establish, we must be careful to communicate them to children in ways that do not threaten their self-esteem. Some frequently used methods can be very destructive to self-esteem. Consider the effects of the following messages:

*How many times do I have to tell you...?* Blame and criticism almost always follow these words. For example: How many times do you have to be reminded to dress yourself on time? Are you hearing impaired or just stupid? As a result, the child feels humiliated, embarrassed and angry.

*Why can't you be like...?* No two children are exactly alike. There really is reason to rejoice in the special uniqueness that each child brings. Making comparisons between siblings or children in groups almost always increases natural rivalries and can lead to lasting resentments.

The child who receives the comparison hears it as "I'm not good enough." The child who's being used for the comparison may learn to see her- or himself as good enough only if she or he is better than someone else. As parents, teachers and caregivers, we need to convey messages that help children to value themselves.

Instead of making comparisons, say what you really want from a child. Do you want better table manners, better study habits, a neater room? A good alternative is to use I-statements (discussed in Chapter 3) to get your point across effectively.

**Labeling or pigeonholing.** Kids are more than their labels. Telling children that one is the beauty, another is the athlete, another shouldn't worry about his or her looks because he or she has the brains, can be extremely limiting. We want to encourage children to develop their talents, but we do not want to define their ambitions too soon. The beauty may also be the brain. The musician might become the mathematician.

Hanging negative labels on children is even more harmful. *Lazy* and *stupid* are two common labels. In schools, we often label kids behavior disordered or learning disabled. We may say a child has an attention deficit disorder. Then we act surprised when these children get even worse. Many learn to live up (or down) to their label. This effect is known as a self-fulfilling prophecy.

—OVERCOMING A LABEL—

Steve was recently labeled an emotionally disturbed student. This eight year old did some very strange things during his first few days in his special education classroom. His teacher, a veteran of 15 years, asked him why he was acting the way he did.

Steve replied, "Because I'm emotionally disturbed." It was as if the label gave him permission to act crazy.

This teacher paused, looked Steve square in the eye, put her arm around him and said, "In this class, everyone is labeled emotionally disturbed. That label is no excuse here." She then proceeded to establish high but reachable expectations for Steve, which he achieved. He left that class after one year.

*How could you be so...?* As caregivers, we can have powerful effects on children's self-esteem. We must remember that these effects can extend beyond the immediate behavior that requires discipline.

Children are embarrassed or humiliated by put-downs. Even if we succeed in getting the child to do as we wish this time, the price paid is an assault to self-confidence, which can lead to long-term feelings of discouragement (I'm not good enough) and anger.

*I'm sick of looking at you!* What a child hears in this message is this person hates me, I'm worthless. This kind of message is an expression of anger. It is much better to say, "Sometimes I feel very angry with you, and right now is one of those times."

*Shut up!* Researchers have noted that words such as these give children the impression that their opinions are not valued. If the phrase is heard often enough, children begin to view themselves as people who have nothing of importance to offer.

## Telling and Showing

Discipline really means teaching. Therefore, strategies and techniques for teaching children about rules need to match children's learning styles. We think that the following activities and strategies can assist you in showing and telling children what is expected in different situations.

*Make your rules clear and specific.* Rules must be as clear and understandable as possible. Statements such as you never listen, your room is a mess—clean it up, put your toys away after you finish playing, are neither clear nor specific enough for most children to understand unless they first break the rule, get caught and then get punished. Avoid situations where children need to break the rules in order to find out what you actually mean.

—WHAT DOES *CLEAN* MEAN?—

Take the situation in which six-year-old Bobby's room is a mess. His father sees toys lying around and clothes strewn all over. Company is coming tonight, and Father wants the room to be tidy. He says, "Bobby, clean up your room, and don't come out until it is tidy."

Bobby goes to his room, spends 15 minutes cleaning, comes out, plops himself on the couch and starts watching TV. Father asks if his room is clean. Bobby says yes.

Father goes upstairs to check. He notices that a few toys are put away, but many are not. The bed is unmade. Dirty clothes have been moved from all over the room to a pile in the corner.

Father comes down and says angrily, "Bobby, what's wrong with you? I'll tolerate no lying. You told me your room was clean, but it's still a mess. Get up there right now and finish the job, or there'll be no TV for two days."

Bobby dejectedly hangs his head as he walks upstairs, confused and unsure about what Father really wants.

Before Father assumes that Bobby was simply lazy, he should make sure that the directions he gave were clear. This means that Father must let Bobby know exactly what Father means when he says clean your room.

Let's see what Father can do when he sees discipline as teaching rather than punishing. Father approaches Bobby and says, "Bobby, company is coming tonight, and your room needs to be cleaned. That means put toys on the shelf, put dirty clothes in the hamper and make the bed."

If Bobby still doesn't get the job done, we realize that Bobby may be like many children who require that we show them what we mean. If

Bobby's room is still untidy after Father's clear and specific directions, then Father needs to take time to show Bobby what he means by *clean*.

Father repeats the direction, goes with Bobby to his room and begins to show Bobby where the toys and clothes need to go. When Father sees that Bobby gets the idea, he provides encouragement and tells Bobby he'll be back in a few minutes to see how Bobby's doing.

Father returns a few moments later, sees Bobby busily at work, offers genuine appreciation and moves on. Once Bobby has had some practice, Father will probably need to say only a few words, such as "Bobby, please clean your room."

Being clear and specific means:

- Tell the child exactly what you want. (The room needs cleaning. That means toys on the shelf, etc.)

- Explain why it is important. (Company is coming.)

- Show the child what you mean. (Help the child get started.)

- Provide genuine appreciation and support when the child follows through.

- Check back occasionally.

- Use one or two words once the skill is learned. (Bobby, please clean your room.)

***Don't blame, teach.*** I was watching my son at a school assembly recently. Certificates were being given out for accomplishments. I noticed that as my son was greeted by the school principal, he made no eye contact. He seemed to extend his hand like a wet noodle. I could feel myself become embarrassed and mad, wondering why my son wasn't showing better manners.

I could hear the voice of criticism and blame rise up inside me. Fortunately, it fell, because my son was sitting far away from me. When I thought about it a bit more, I realized that I had neither shown nor taught my son how to shake hands appropriately, nor had I explained the importance of greeting someone with eye contact.

I was expecting my son to behave in a way that he had been neither taught nor shown. Yet, when he proved to be an unsuccessful reader of his father's mind, I was mad. My son needed to be taught, not blamed.

It is important that we view children's misbehavior, misdeeds or mis-understandings as opportunities to teach and explain rather than as times to yell, put down or criticize.

***Have high expectations.*** Developing good discipline is a slow process. The final goal is that children will be able to make wise, responsible choices that will lead to success in life. Children need to learn early that they are not the only people with needs. They must learn to contribute to the well-being of the family or school class by assuming responsibilities appropriate to their ages and stages of development.

Parents and teachers do children a major disservice when they allow responsibilities to be shirked or when they permit insulting, willful and disobedient behavior. Kids need to be given responsibility, and they need to be clearly confronted in a dignified way when they act-up.

Young children who are allowed to be verbally abusive, to break the rules without consequences, or who are given no responsibility, turn into resentful, angry teenagers and adults. They feel little compassion for the needs of others. Children without limits and those who are victims of harshness become tomorrow's delinquents.

In addition to providing children with work to do and placing a value on the importance of school, you must also feel comfortable confronting children when they get out of hand.

Get close to the child, look directly into his or her eyes and firmly express your dissatisfaction. Use as few words as necessary to communicate your concern. Tell the child exactly what you want him or her to do the next time he or she is in a similar situation. Finally, ask the child to repeat what he or she will do differently next time. Offer a smile and a way-to-go when the child seems to get it.

You may need to do this several times, particularly with children who have a more difficult temperament. Having high expectations means:

- Expect responsible behavior early in life by assigning jobs and expecting them to be done well.

- Expect respectful behavior from children.

- When unacceptable behavior occurs, firmly express your displeasure. Get close to the child and use eye contact. (Do not demand eye contact. Some cultures frown on children making eye contact with adults. It is viewed as a sign of disrespect.)

- Let your displeasure sink in. Then tell the child how to express him- or herself more acceptably in the future.

- You may need to repeat these steps several times.

# Modeling

The most powerful way to get kids to behave is to model what you want. Lisa brought her eight-year-old son, Robert, for counseling because he kept hitting other kids, including his siblings, when he didn't get what he wanted.

Lisa was exasperated. No matter how much she talked to Robert about sharing and not hitting, it wasn't getting through. Observations of Robert with his parents found that spankings were often used when talking didn't work.

Neither Lisa nor her husband realized that they were modeling aggressive behavior by spanking their son. Robert was using a similar behavior when he sought power with his playmates and siblings. The old cliché that actions speak louder than words is really a principle of effective discipline.

As parents and teachers, we must examine and reexamine our attitudes and beliefs. Most importantly, we must be ever aware of our own behavior and its effects on children.

Telling kids not to hit other people flies in the face of reason when we spank them. Reminding kids to say please and thank you will generally fall on deaf ears unless they hear you using these words both with them and with others.

Children are more likely to keep things clean and orderly when parents and teachers are themselves organized about their own belongings. Children will be more likely to compliment others when they themselves are complimented. And they are much more likely to develop a spirit of sharing when you share with them rather than criticize when they don't share with others.

If we don't want kids to smoke, drink or use drugs, how are we as adults doing with those substances? If we want kids to be honest, do we lie to them? Do we tell them to forgive others while we model keeping grudges? Effective discipline requires that we practice and demonstrate what we preach.

# Chapter 3

# Communicating

Communication is critical to the success of any relationship. We communicate our thoughts and feelings in a variety of ways. While words and language are important to communication, tone of voice, how we hold our body and facial expression transmit more than 90 percent of the message. *How* we say something is often more important than *what* we say.

How we communicate thus determines the effectiveness and appropriateness of discipline. We need and want to get a message across, but we must do it in a way that maintains a child's dignity and self-esteem.

# Listening

Listening is a difficult skill. Everyone wants to be listened to; everyone agrees they should listen to others. Yet, effective listening is rare. Every parent and teacher has heard the accusation, "You never listen to me!" Every parent or teacher has said to a child, "You don't listen to me."

Listening is one of the most important human relations skills. The relationship between adults and children intensifies the need for listening. When we listen to children, we offer the following benefits:

- We show children that we care.
- We dignify children.
- We give children a chance to express thoughts and feelings.
- We let children know they are important.
- We model listening skills for children.

Why is it so difficult to listen? There are many reasons, including the following:

- competition for our attention from other stimulation, thoughts, worries and problems
- short attention spans

- the temptation to judge what the other person is saying rather than to hear it

- the rehearsing syndrome, when we rehearse how and what we will say next rather than hearing the speaker

- impatience

- lack of understanding

- unwillingness to acknowledge the other person's thoughts and feelings, especially when we disagree

Some people are toppers. They top what you say with a bigger story of their own. You have a cold; they have pneumonia. You won a game; they won a tournament. You found a bargain; they beat your price by 30 percent.

Other people are breath watchers. They wait until you pause to take a breath, and then change the subject. What they have to say is always more important than what you have to say.

The skill of listening takes effort, but it is well worth it. Listening, as much as any human relation skill, is a pure sign of caring. When children know that parents and teachers truly care, discipline is easier. Here are some guidelines for effective listening.

***Clear your head.*** Empty other thoughts from your head, so they don't interfere with what you are hearing. When you find yourself thinking of other things, simply go back to listening. If you miss something, it is better to ask the child to repeat it than to pretend to hear.

For example, you might say: "I'm sorry. I missed what you just said. It's important for me to understand you, so I would like you to say it one more time for me."

***Focus.*** Listening requires concentration. There can be many distractions. At home, they may include television, phone calls or something burning on the stove. At school, the distractions may be other children, student papers to read, or a meeting to attend.

When you need to listen to a child, try to give the child your full attention. You can't really hear what is being said when the background is full of noise.

**Defer judgment.** Prejudgment is a filter that interferes with the ability to take in information and truly hear it. When you are listening, don't judge what you hear as either right or wrong, true or false or important or trivial. Simply try to understand it. That can be tough, especially when blame is coming your way.

—THE SHOPPING TRIP—

Mom and Kaprisha are at a store when Kaprisha shows Mom new Barbie clothes she wants. Mom tells her that they are too expensive and that she doesn't have the money right now. Kaprisha scowls and says, "You always buy Anthony (brother) whatever he wants—that's not fair!"

Mom is tempted to say defensively, "Stop complaining! That's not true and you know it! Just last week I bought you a scooter." Instead, she decides to listen. She says, "You feel disappointed and angry because you really want those clothes. Even though I bought you a new scooter last week, I know it hurts when you can't get something you want."

**Empathize.** Put yourself in the speaker's place. Imagine yourself in that situation. Live the story as it is described to you. When the speaker has finished, you may want to relate a similar situation from your experience to show that you can relate empathetically to what you heard. Don't try to top the original story, and don't shift the focus to your agenda or problem.

For example: When your child says, "Billy hit me first," don't quickly assume you are hearing an excuse. Listen carefully, ask questions and then come to a conclusion.

—WHAT'S FOR DINNER?—

Connie: Mom, I never get to choose what's for dinner.

Mom: Gee, Connie, I didn't realize that mattered to you. I don't like it either when I don't have any choices. We could do one or both of the following: You can pick dinner one night a week and I'll make it, or you can fix yourself something to eat when you don't like what's for dinner.

**Rephrase.** When the speaker is finished, rephrase what was said in your own words. This ensures that you have actually heard what was said, and lets the speaker know you have heard it.

—It's Not Fair—

Anita: It's not fair! Why do I have to do what you say just because you're my father?

Dad: When you disagree, you don't think it's fair that you should have to do it my way just because I'm your father. Is that what you're saying?

**Be patient.** Don't cut in or cut the speaker off. Don't say anything until the speaker has finished.

**Ask probing questions.** To be sure you understand and to give the speaker a chance to think further about the subject, ask thought-provoking questions. Do not conduct an inquisition. The questions should provoke thought, not imply guilt or accuse.

For example, say: "Can you think of any reason your teacher might have been angry with you?" rather than "Your teacher must have had a reason for being angry. Tell me what it is." Or say, "Why do you think you got a *D*?" rather than "I told you that your laziness would catch up with you."

**State your side.** When it is your turn to speak, tell the other person how you feel or what you think without negating what you have heard.

For example, say: "I see it a little differently than you do. I feel that children should go to bed earlier than adults because..."; rather than "You're wrong. You will go to bed when I tell you."

_____ *Am I in Trouble?*

***Allow and acknowledge the expression of feelings.*** When children say they are angry or upset, don't discourage them from talking about it. One of the most positive ways to deal with feelings is to simply hear them. There is nothing wrong with any feeling. Good discipline helps children learn how to control their behavior. We can't nor should we require that children control their feelings. It is OK to feel hurt, but it is not OK to hurt others.

Healthy emotional development encourages children to talk about their feelings, rather than to act on them by hurting people or breaking rules.

—EXPRESSING FEELINGS—

When Billy does something to make you mad, tell Billy you are angry; it's not OK to hit him.

You sound upset right now, and you have every right to be. I understand why you feel that way. I sometimes get upset, too. What do you think are some things you could do or say when Phyllis and Maria call you names?

When listening, try to establish the best possible conditions to facilitate successful communication. Cut down on outside distractions. Be sure you have enough time to communicate. The way you listen will play a large part in how the tone is set for communication.

Sometimes you must go out of your way to listen to children. Once you get over the inertia and natural resistance to change, you will find that successful communication is worth the price you pay for it. The following are some of the conditions for effective listening.

***Remove distractions.*** Turn off the television and the stereo. Find a place where you can be alone with the child. Tell others that you are not to be disturbed for a while.

***Provide adequate time.*** Ask or estimate how much time the child needs to explain the situation to you. Then plan for at least 50 percent more time. Don't look at your watch or get antsy. Don't hurry the child.

Don't try to resolve a difficult situation in two minutes. You might have to schedule another time to listen if there is too much to cover in one session. It's better to leave things undecided than to reach a hasty answer.

***Sit at the child's level.*** Don't stand over the child. Standing puts you in a physically superior position and can cut the communication process short.

***Set up regular discussion times.*** This can work in a family or in a class. Try to find time to talk on a regular basis, both as a group and individually. You may want to have formal weekly meetings. Some families reserve dinnertime for discussion.

Be sure that everyone has a chance to say what is on her or his mind. An important part of listening is to have the opportunity to be heard. Prevention is always easier than cure. Providing time to speak before there is a problem is always easier than coping after a problem escalates into something bigger.

Listening isn't always easy, especially when we have a point to make or want to be heard. However, listening might make the difference between a smoothly functioning family or class, which has the ability to solve problems and resolve differences, and one always on the verge of explosion.

## I-Statements

The importance of body language and tone of voice in communication has already been discussed. Eighty to ninety percent of our communication both to children and to other adults occurs through body language and tone of voice.

But that still leaves ten to twenty percent of the message to be expressed by the words we use. And the words we use, when combined with our tone of voice and body language, determine whether we'll be heard and respected, heard and resented, ignored, or ignored and resented.

As a rule of thumb, we need to deal with children when they misbehave in the same way we would want someone to deal with us if they thought we needed correcting. Just imagine that your manager comes to you at the end of the day because the work you were supposed to have finished by day's end didn't get done. Little does she realize that the phone rang off the hook and a hundred other important matters needed attention.

As you start explaining, she bellows (in front of your co-workers), "I'm sick of the excuses. I don't pay you good money to sit around here and not get it done."

Now, even if the work could have gotten done, does that manager have any right to treat you that way in front of other workers? How would you feel? Even if you stayed longer to get the work done, you would probably feel humiliated, embarrassed, resentful and angry.

Now suppose instead that your manager either asks you into her office or invites you to a place away from fellow employees. She says, "I feel upset and frustrated because I expected the job to be done by today and it isn't."

As you explain the busyness of the day, she says, "I didn't realize you had so many important things to do today. It must have been hectic. Will you be able to get that project done by tonight or tomorrow morning?"

This manager has made it clear that the job is very important, but she has treated you with dignity and respect. She has made her complaint in private to avoid embarrassing you. She has heard you express how harried you felt, which helps you feel understood. And she has used I-statements.

In a nonblaming but clear and concise manner, the manager let you know what she felt. She began her sentence with *I* rather than a blaming *you*. She then gave the reason for her feelings (not always easy to do), and ended the encounter by seeking a plan. (Will this get done tonight or tomorrow?)

The wise parent or teacher, like the wise manager, looks beyond the immediate moment of frustration and overcomes the temptation to react with blame and anger. To truly influence children, you must be able to communicate in a way that makes it likely that your intentions, feelings and thoughts are being understood.

When expressing your feelings as part of discipline, it is helpful to think in terms of *you-statements* and *I-statements*.

A you-statement conveys some combination of lecture, criticism, sarcasm, threat or scolding. Even when these messages work (stop misbehavior), they have the negative effect of eroding a child's self-esteem.

—SOME YOU–STATEMENTS—

Phillip, you are being a very bad boy. You shouldn't touch the expensive furniture. If you don't stop, you'll be sorry!

Sally, your loud laughing and silliness are driving me crazy. Talk like the big girl you are, not like a baby.

Jodie, not sharing that book with Kirby is very selfish.

Carl, you keep leaving your toys around like a slob. I've told you before to pick them up. I know you can hear. Don't you pretend to be deaf, young man!

In each of these examples, the child is being blamed, criticized or threatened. The solution that is either given or implied is do it my way or else.

As responsible parents and educators, we need to keep in mind that the real goal of discipline is to teach the child *self*-discipline. When children know that parents or teachers will solve problems, then they don't have to think for themselves.

I-statements provide a way for you, as a parent or teacher, to let the child know clearly and specifically but nonaccusingly how you feel about what the child did or did not do. Then you can work with the child to devise a better solution to the problem.

Let's go back to the examples and use constructive rather than destructive language to communicate feelings and expectations.

—Using I–Statements—

Phillip, I am really worried that touching will scratch and ruin that expensive furniture.

Sally, I'm working with the reading group, and I need to have quiet so I can hear them read.

Jodie, I'm disappointed that the book I bought for all of us to read is not getting shared. Do you have any solutions to my problem?

Carl, I'm really afraid that someone in this family whom I love is going to trip and be hurt on one of the toys that are lying around. What can you do about that?

Can you see the differences between these two ways of talking or correcting? I-statements convey respect and dignity to the child, because the parent or teacher takes responsibility or owns his or her feelings. The child is viewed as capable of contributing valuable solutions to the problem.

Practicing I-statements and then using them allows us to get away from such standard lines as "If you do that one more time, I'll..."; "Stop behaving like a lousy, rotten kid"; or "You stupid jerk!" Be careful when you use I-statements. It can be easy at first to start your sentence with *I* but to criticize, blame or threaten anyway. For example: I feel sad when *you act like a jerk.* I am sick and tired of *raising a slob.*

An I-statement is effective because:

ෂ	It says how you feel when a child does or does not do something.

ෂ	It gives a reason.

ෂ	It never labels the child (e.g., jerk, stupid, idiot, useless, etc.).

ෂ	It invites the child to solve the problem.

When you aren't home on time, I feel worried that something terrible has happened to you.

Carlos, it's important to me that I do this job well and finish it soon. Each time you interrupt me, I forget where I was, and I'm afraid I'll make a mistake. We'll talk after I've finished.

Janice, when your teacher tells me that your homework isn't turned in on time, I feel disappointed and kind of sad. I have a lot of pride in you. Help me understand what the problem is.

Getting good at using I-statements, like many of the activities in this book, requires practice. Next time you feel like yelling at a child, take a few deep breaths. Then express your feelings with I-statements. See what happens when you persist in doing this with children.

I-statements give you an opportunity to be clear in telling children how you feel, without feeling guilty afterward about the way you expressed yourself.

## The Broken Record

If something is important to you, then you need to be prepared to persist in communicating its importance to the children you deal with. With some challenging or headstrong children, the broken record approach and related methods of persistence are very useful in changing behavior.

Parents and teachers of such children often give up too easily. They have the correct technique or way of communicating, but when it doesn't work immediately, they become discouraged. Then they resort to old methods that have proven ineffective over time.

The broken record technique is to say what you want several times in a persistent manner. This tells the child that you are serious about seeing that your expectations are met. Simply say and do the same thing over and over again until the message gets through.

At the same time, be sure to use I-statements, keep your anger and frustration under control, and express yourself matter of factly.

—Nick's Story—

Let's say that one of Nick's jobs is to empty the trash. If Nick is like most kids, the trash could be overflowing into his bed before he paid it any attention.

His parent says, "Nick, after breakfast, the trash needs to be emptied." Breakfast comes and goes, and still the trash remains. Parent says assertively, without anger, "Nick, the trash needs emptying."

Nick says, "Yeah, yeah, I know. I'll do it!" An hour later the trash is still there.

After school Nick comes home. After afternoon greetings, Mom says, "Nick, the trash needs emptying."

Nick says, "Yeah, I'll get to it."

Mom is moderately frustrated when she sees Nick an hour later, and the trash is still not emptied. She decides to try the broken record one last time. She says, "Nick, the garbage needs emptying. I'm frustrated and angry that this is the fourth time I've made that request with no result."

If that does not motivate Nick to do the job, then Nick needs to be shown that Mom means business. When you begin reasonable persistence efforts at an early age, most kids get the message by the second or third broken record message that they need to get the job done.

But some kids have more challenging temperaments or have come to believe that the world owes them something. They need actions to follow the words. The actions should be related to the rule that has been broken, and should be designed to teach better behavior rather than relying on punishment.

—Nick's Story—Continued—

In Nick's case, Mother decides that since there isn't enough

Communicating _____ 37

room to empty the dinner's trash because the old trash remains, she'll need to cook less food. Therefore, she'll cook only for those who fulfill their family obligations. She serves dinner in the usual manner. But when Nick sits down to eat, there is no food for him.

Nick looks quizzically at Mom, certain that this was either an oversight or Mom has suddenly lost a few marbles. He says, "Mom, where's my dinner?"

Mom, in a calm, matter-of-fact, dignified way, says, "I will neither cook nor clean up after anyone in the family who refuses to do his work around here."

Nick's mother has clearly communicated her message, without blame, criticism or threats. We can't guarantee that Nick will take out the garbage even now, but he has the opportunity to learn a valuable lesson.

# Chapter 4

# **Empowering**

How much power do children have? How much power do children need? Children learn quickly how to get what they want. Babies learn that crying can get them all sorts of things, from bottles to hugs. Toddlers learn that being stubborn may result in a tired parent or frazzled caregiver giving in to demands.

A conflict ensues when a parent, teacher or caregiver gets tired of the child's demands and of the child's method of making the demands. For much of the child/parent relationship, the issue of power is a major source of conflict and confusion.

Power is also an important issue in the classroom and in childcare situations. Each child wants to control the environment, to have and do what he or she wants, to make others do as directed. Parents, teachers and caregivers want children to do as they are told.

Most children need and want limits; they do not feel comfortable with unlimited freedom or choices. Parents and educators also want children to become responsible, thinking people who can make good decisions by themselves.

In the context of family, empowerment involves the process of defining what the child can and cannot control. Children learn about control and power in a variety of ways. They learn by modeling what they see their parents and siblings do.

Dolls, play figures and other toys and games encourage children to roleplay real-life situations that allow them to act like adults in control. This kind of play helps children learn how to control their environment. Games like house and school and work allow children to experience the power of making adult-like decisions.

Empowerment is difficult for parents and teachers to manage because control is a basic human need. The adult's need for control conflicts with the child's need to feel powerful or in control. No matter how young the child is, the desire for self-control is a powerful determinant of behavior.

Children, even young ones, demand the right to make choices about their own behavior. This creates a dilemma. If we allow too many choices or total freedom, children can become uncontrollable and can hurt themselves.

If we allow too few choices, children may become too compliant, learn to be dependent, and even become helpless. These children learn not to think. Children who are continually denied an opportunity to make choices often rebel as soon as the need for power becomes stronger than the need for approval.

The issue of empowerment is about deciding how many choices to give young children, when to start giving choices, and how to give choices in a way most likely to help children learn to be responsible.

# Locus of Control

*Locus of control* is a term used by psychologists and educators to refer to control of behavior. Understanding this concept can help us teach children about responsibility and choices. Locus of control studies define two possible places of control.

***Internal locus of control.*** Individuals are responsible for what happens to them in any given situation. Control is within the person.

—SOME INTERNAL SITUATIONS—

You are late for an important appointment because you decided to stop at a store to get one last errand done before your appointment.

Your child has a messy room because he or she threw toys and clothes all over the floor.

A child does poorly on a test and believes that the bad performance is because he or she didn't study the materials.

A student turns a worksheet in late because he or she was playing during work time.

***External locus of control.*** Forces outside the individual's control cause things to happen.

—SOME EXTERNAL SITUATIONS—

You are late for an important appointment because you are caught in a traffic jam with no way to get out.

Your child has a messy room because his or her brother and sister threw toys and clothes all over the floor.

A child does poorly on a test because the material is too difficult for him or her.

A student turns a worksheet in late because there were too many questions to answer in the time available.

According to locus of control theory, the following conditions explain how children learn to be responsible.

If the situation is internal, that is, if the situation is in the control of the child, then the child should have an *internal orientation*. This means that the child recognizes that she or he caused what happened.

If the child perceives the locus of control to be external, then she or he will blame other people or events and believe that the problem is not her or his fault. We've all experienced the range of excuses kids give when they don't want to take responsibility.

- It's not my fault.
- He did it first.
- It just broke.

In order to change their behavior, children need an internal orientation. They must believe that change is possible through their own actions.

Our role as parents and educators is to help children be aware of how their actions create outcomes. Then the child will be internally focused and can deal with the problem. The following example shows how to help children move from an external to an internal orientation, so behavior can change.

Parent or teacher: You forgot to do your homework.

Child: It wasn't my fault. Billy asked me to play with him. He made me forget.

Parent or teacher: You mean when you played with Billy, you forgot to do your homework?

Child: Yeah, Billy made me forget.

Parent or teacher: What can you do the next time Billy asks you to play, so you won't forget to do your homework?

Child: I'll tell him I have to do my homework first.

If the situation is external, that is, if the situation is out of the control of the child, then the child should have an *external orientation*. He or she will correctly understand that his or her behavior or choices were not responsible for the outcome.

If children perceive the locus of control to be internal, when it is actually external, they feel guilt and a sense of failure for not being able to do something that they really cannot do.

Think of a Little Leaguer who lacks the ability to hit the ball. Telling this child to try harder will not increase his or her skill. It will only make the child feel embarrassed and stupid. The adult's role in this case is to let the child know that he or she did the best he or she could and shouldn't feel bad about the result.

We should be careful about asking children to do things beyond their control. Telling a child to do a good job sweeping the floor will do no good unless you show the child how to sweep and just what a good job is.

—YOU DID YOUR BEST—

Child: I'm sorry I only cleaned up part of my room.

Parent: How much did you do?

Child: I put my clothes away, but not all my toys.

Parent: You only had about a half hour. I watched you and saw that you worked the whole time. No one can ask you to do more than try. I'm proud of your effort. Next time we'll figure a way to plan for more time.

Teachers can apply this example to a child who doesn't complete an assignment and interprets that as failure. Encourage these children, and help them match tasks to their abilities.

Let's examine a more complicated situation and notice how locus of control influences what a child learns.

—It's Dinner Time—

A child repeatedly comes late to dinner. Here are three possible reasons that the child might not be responsible:

1. Dinner time consistently changes, so the child is never sure when she or he is expected to be at the dinner table.

2. The parent yells to the child, who is in the middle of an activity (reading, listening to music, playing a game), "Dinner, wash up and come to the table right now." The child has little or no advance warning and no time to shift gears.

3. The child has not been taught the concept of time management, so she or he has not learned to be on time. Telling time and using time are different skills.

If any of the above situations exist, the child is simply not able to come to the table on time. The expectation will not be met, and it is not the child's fault. The best way to improve the child's lateness is to:

1. Have dinner at a regular time so the child can *predict* when he or she is expected and can *plan* to be there on time.

2. Give the child enough time to finish what he or she is doing. It is not reasonable to expect a child to drop everything at a

moment's notice. Think how angry you feel when a child demands something of you when you are in the middle of something else.

3. Teach the child both how to tell time and how to use time. Explain that if dinnertime is at 6:00 P.M., then he or she should start wrapping up his or her activities at 5:45, not at 6:00. In a classroom, teach children how to predict and plan to be ready for recess.

When children are punished for what they cannot control or influence, they become helpless, angry and powerless. They no longer feel good about who they are, and they lose the ability to become responsible for their behavior.

Extreme instances can lead to serious emotional problems. Drug use and symptoms of stress are two possible reactions that can occur when children simply cannot handle the pressure of too-high expectations.

When we teach children to be responsible, we help them make good choices when the situation is internal, and help them cope when the situation is external.

We need to recognize when the demands are beyond the ability of the child, and modify them or provide instruction or assistance when needed. However, we should not do for the child what the child can do for her- or himself.

## Skills for Responsibility

There are three skills associated with developing an internal orientation—predicting, choosing and planning.

*Predicting.* In order to be responsible, children need to understand that certain behaviors bring predictable results. If children can make no connection between what they do and what happens next, then no learning can occur. Life becomes a game of chance.

You can use *predicting* to improve discipline in two ways.

1. Be predictable. If you say you will do something, do it. Keep your promises. Keep things relatively on schedule. Exceptions are OK, because the world is not always perfect. (Give an explanation if you can.) But when exceptions occur too frequently, children begin to see the world as random, like a lottery.

2. Ask children lots of predicting questions.

—SOME PREDICTION QUESTIONS—

What do you think your sister will do if you give her half of your orange? (Don't ask this in a preachy way.)

What do you think will happen if you give your mother (or father) a hug?

What do you think will happen if you hit your brother?

What do you think will happen if you clean your room? if you don't clean your room?

What do you think will happen if people keep throwing erasers?

What do you think will happen if you keep picking on the other kids?

These kinds of questions work best when they are asked not as a threat, but to help children understand what might happen in the future. Your tone of voice, timing and emotional state when asking will determine if the questions will be perceived as a threat or not.

*Choosing.* In order to be responsible, children must have more than one choice. In addition, the options have to be real and feel like choices. Imagine you are walking down a street and someone points a gun to your head and says, "Your money or your life."

You respond, "How can you do that to me!"

He or she answers, "I'm being very humanistic. I'm giving you a choice."

A choice between *doing things your way* and a *punishment* feels the same to a child as your choices would if there was a gun to your head. You may get the child to do what you want, but you do not teach responsibility.

When children are given real choices, there is no guarantee they will want any of them. But it's a beginning for learning how to be responsible.

—THE CHOICE IS...—

You can clean up your mess right now, or you can do it in half an hour.

You can go to the store with me if you don't whine, or you can stay here with your sister.

You can get dressed before I drive you to daycare, or you can go in your pajamas.

You can do the first five math problems or the last five.

When you are angry, you can tell how you feel, write a note or hit the pillow in the back of the classroom.

You can do the work in class, during recess or after school.

*Planning.* The better you are able to plan, the more likely you are to control what happens to you. Plans such as shopping lists (they help you get what you want at the supermarket), recipes (they help you get what you want when you cook), maps and directions to a new place (they help you get where you want to go) and budgets (they help you keep track of the money you have to spend) all help you get what you want.

The better you are at planning and at following your plans, the more responsible you can be for what happens to you. You can use planning as a teaching tool. Ask children how they plan to meet their goals.

—HELP CHILDREN PLAN—

John, how can you earn enough money to buy that new action figure you want?

Sarah, how can you get your room clean before Grandma comes over tomorrow to visit?

Raymond, how can you improve enough to score a goal in soccer?

Cassandra, what can you do to let Richard know that taking your book makes you angry?

Each of these three skills—predicting, choosing and planning—can be taught to children as part of a program for discipline. And as you will see later, these skills become the basis for logical consequences.

It is important to keep in mind that in spite of good predicting, choosing and planning skills, life is full of unexpected circumstances. John Lennon once said, "Life is what happens when you're busy making other plans." But these skills will help children learn what can and can't be controlled, and how to become responsible for what can be controlled.

## Guidelines for Control

There are many factors in determining how much control children should have. Some general guidelines are:

*Safety first.* When safety or danger are involved, children's choices are highly limited. Children should not have a choice to play with stoves, matches, electrical outlets, medicines, household chemicals or anything that may hurt them.

While this principle might seem obvious, parents sometimes give mixed messages by not being firm and clear enough about the limits.

—An Inappropriate Message—

James, don't you want to leave that outlet alone?

—An Appropriate Message—

James, do not touch that outlet. (Adult takes the child's hand away from the cord.)

***Don't do for children what they can do for themselves.*** Many times we try to solve children's problems for them when they are perfectly able to solve their own. Encouraging children to solve their own problems not only gives them a sense of confidence, but also a sense of power and their ability to master their environment.

—An Inappropriate Response—

Julio (whining and tattling to an adult): Daniel took my pencil.

Adult: He did, did he? Well, I'm going to take that pencil away from him right now.

—An Appropriate Response—

Adult: I'm glad he didn't take mine. Then I'd have to find a way to get it back. Now you have to do it. What are you going to do?

If the child chooses an unacceptable alternative, the skills of *predicting* and *planning* can refocus the child's choice.

—Helping the Child Make an Appropriate Choice—

Julio: I'm going to smack him in the head, that's what.

Adult: What do you think will happen if you smack him?

Julio: He'll smack me back.

Adult: Then what will happen?

Julio: We'll have a fight.

Adult: Will you get your pencil back that way?

Julio: No. He'll never give it back.

Adult: What else can you do?

Julio: I can tell him to give it to me.

Adult: That might work. Why not try it and tell me what happens?

*All children need choices.* The number of choices depends on the age of the child. Young children can usually handle no more than two or three choices: You can have a tuna fish or peanut butter and jelly sandwich. Older children can handle many more: Why don't you look in the refrigerator and see what you want for lunch?

The appropriate amount of choices is usually more than what adults want and less than what children want.

**Be experimental.** Learn from your mistakes, and let children learn from theirs. Don't be afraid to give up a little control in small amounts and see what happens. Many of the fears you have may not be realized.

Children can actually make well-thought-out decisions when given the chance to do so. When children make choices that turn out badly, you can help more by helping them make better choices next time than by criticizing or ridiculing them.

Power comes from the ability to make decisions and do things on our own, from learning how to be internal when the situation is within our ability to control.

—TAKE THE BUS—

When my son was in seventh grade, I drove him to school every day. But he always had to take public transportation home. When he wanted to go to the store or to a friend's house during the day, he also had to take the bus.

He often complained and called me a terrible father, because I didn't drive him around all the time like the parents of his friends. As he grew older, he learned to use public transportation to get around the city. Eventually, he was able to take visitors to the well-known tourist spots for me, so I didn't always have to go.

When he was a junior in high school, he thanked me. I asked, "For what?"

He said, "For not driving me around all the time."

I was very surprised by his thanks, so I asked him to explain his change of heart.

"All my friends want to go to a movie," he said, "but we have no one to drive us. I said we should take the bus, but none of them knew how. I couldn't believe that a kid my age didn't know how to use a bus. Then I realized that my friends never had to. I appreciate you for making me learn to do it myself. Now, I think my friends are helpless and I'm not. That's why I'm thanking you."

My son had been empowered by my insistence that he learn to navigate the city on his own.

# Chapter 5

# Consequences
# and Punishments

Throughout this book, we advocate treating children with respect and dignity. In order to be responsible and make good decisions, children need to feel good about themselves and have good people skills, including the ability to understand how it feels to be in someone else's shoes. Children also need to know acceptable ways to handle stressful feelings and how to plan.

As parents and educators, we want to encourage behavior that reflects these skills and discourage behavior that doesn't demonstrate them. When a child tells another that he or she is angry, he or she is effectively using a responsible communication skill to express his or her feelings. We want to encourage that. When a child bites, hits, slaps or grabs another, he or she hasn't learned the appropriate skill and can only express frustration about failing to get what he or she wants.

When a child breaks a rule, the parent or teacher intervenes. Interventions, or responses, can be either consequences or punishments.

Punishments teach children to obey by making them feel bad about what they have done, with the hope that they will not want to do those things again. Punishments include spankings, threats, loss of privileges, lectures, scolding and sarcasm. Punishments, which hurt the child in some way, often cause short-term behavior change. Over time, however, punishments lead to greater problems.

Consequences teach responsibility. They help children learn to make better choices in the future. A consequence should be related to a behavior as directly as possible, so the child sees, feels and experiences the results of his or her behavior.

Consequences that are natural or logical are most likely to teach a child better future behavior, because the child directly sees the connection between what she or he did and what happens. Having no clean clothes when a child does not put the dirty ones in the hamper is a natural outcome of the behavior.

There are times when obedience is essential. When the safety of the child or others is in jeopardy, natural consequences can be too dangerous. For example:

- A child should not have to burn her or his hand to learn not to touch a hot stove.

- A child should not have to get lost to learn not to stray from his or her parents.

- A child should not have to receive a shock to learn not to play with electrical outlets.

## Comparing Consequences and Punishments

Let's look at some of the differences between consequences and punishments.

*Self-respect and dignity.* If you think back to your earliest memories, you will recall learning a great deal from your mistakes. Some of your greatest lessons probably resulted from your biggest mistakes. But certain feelings and actions can prevent children from learning important lessons from their mistakes. These include:

- fear of being severely punished

- fear of being unloved

- fear of looking stupid, dumb or incompetent

- being overly defensive

- blaming someone or something else

In a sense, we can label all these feelings and actions as an expression of the loss of self-esteem, or loss of dignity. Generally speaking, when the fear of loss of dignity is more powerful than the need to grow, children stop learning and start protecting themselves.

They do it any way they can. The techniques of protection are familiar to all of us—lying, bragging, not listening, not trying, always asking for help even when it's not needed, bullying, showing off and many others.

Attacks on the dignity of children are felt as punishments. Interventions that enhance children's dignity are consequences. To help understand how powerful dignity is, simply think back on your school days.

Recall two teachers—one, a teacher you are still angry at, so that even recalling the teacher's name gets you upset; the other, a teacher you still love and care deeply about. Think about the differences in the way these two teachers treated you. One attacked your dignity; the other enhanced it. If you are like most people, that is the only real difference between these two teachers.

**Power.** Power usually involves choices. Punishments are power based, meaning that the choice belongs to the adult. Locus of control is external to the child. The parent or teacher makes the decision, and the child follows it. Consequences are learning based, meaning that the child has the opportunity to make a choice and to learn from it.

| PUNISHMENT | CONSEQUENCE |
|---|---|
| Mary, your bed is not made. You are going to miss one hour of television. | Mary, your bed is not made. When are you going to make it? |

**Natural and logical vs. arbitrary.** Consequences are natural and/or logical. They are directly related to the rule, and the connection is obvious to the child. Punishments are arbitrary. They are not connected to the rule.

| PUNISHMENT | CONSEQUENCE |
|---|---|
| Adam, you were late for the bus. No desserts for a week. (There is no connection between desserts and the bus.) | Adam, you missed the bus. I guess you'll have to walk to school. (There is a connection between missing the bus and walking to school.) |

***Time focus.*** Punishments look at the past. They are designed to make children feel bad about what they did so they won't do it again. Consequences look to the future. They are designed to teach children to make better decisions.

Punishments typically stop the misbehavior for a short time. Then they teach people to continue misbehaving but to be more careful about getting caught. Most people who receive a speeding ticket will slow down for a couple of hours. Then they will watch for police officers.

Consequences make people think of better ways to do things and have a longer effect. A person who has been in an accident slows down a lot longer than someone who got a speeding ticket.

***Responsibility vs. obedience.*** Consequences teach children to be more responsible. Punishments teach children to be more obedient. The word *responsibility* means *the ability to respond.* Responsible people have the ability to make good decisions. Obedient people do what they are told, because they fear the negative results if they don't.

Internal locus of control is related to responsibility. External locus of control is related to obedience. Therefore, an intervention that is related to an external orientation is a punishment. An intervention related to an internal orientation is a consequence.

A punishment results in the following:

- It usually attacks the dignity of the child.
- It's externally oriented.
- It focuses on the past.
- It gives short-term results, at best.
- It's not related to the rule.

In contrast, a consequence accomplishes the following:

- It usually enhances the dignity of the child.
- It's internally oriented.

- It focuses on the future.
- It gives long-term results.
- It's related to the rule.

—ADULT CONSEQUENCES AND PUNISHMENTS—

You are late at the airport.

*Consequence:* You miss your plane.

*Punishment:* You are asked to go into the baggage room and write "I won't be late for airports" five hundred times.

You forget to buy something you need at the store.

*Consequence:* You go back to the store and buy it.

*Punishment:* You are sent to your room to think about how careless you are.

You serve meat at dinner, even though the friend you've invited for a special occasion is a vegetarian.

*Consequence:* Your friend doesn't eat very much, and you feel terrible. You sincerely apologize and run into the kitchen to fix something special.

*Punishment:* Your friend gives you a scolding or lecture: How many times do I have to tell you that I don't eat meat? Why are you always so careless? Don't you ever think of anyone but yourself? I don't know what your problem is, but you better straighten it out.

Notice how silly these examples would seem if they were to happen to us as adults, but how easy they are to give to children. Yet, children feel the same way we do when punishments like these are given to them.

## Generic Consequences

There are three consequences that can be used when a rule is broken.

These consequences directly relate to locus of control. They are the skills that help children develop an internal locus of control—predicting, choosing and planning.

**Predicting.** Predicting is a modest consequence. It can serve as a warning without threat. Simply ask the child what he or she thinks will happen in the future if he or she repeats the inappropriate activity.

—WHAT IF?—

Thomas, what do you think will happen if you take Brian's game again?

Sarah, what do you think will happen if you refuse to go to bed at your bedtime?

**Choosing.** Choosing means giving the child a choice between two or three acceptable behaviors as an alternative to what the child did that broke a rule.

—CHOICES—

Constance, the next time you are angry with Ana, you may not hit. You can tell her how you feel, you can write down how you feel on a piece of paper, or you can hit your pillow. Which of these will you do?

**Planning.** Planning means asking the child to plan a solution to the problem. This is the most effective consequence in the long term, but it requires that a child be old enough to understand how to plan and what the words mean.

—PLANS—

Chris, what are you going to do to make sure you don't use unacceptable language in class?

Carol, what are you going to do about your things that are left all over the house?

We recommend that if you use plans, you accept any plan the child offers as long as it is a plan and not a promise. Promises such as I will not fight or I will keep the living room clean are highly ineffective. Good plans say exactly what the child will do. For example: I will tell how I feel with my words, not with my fists. I will put all my things in my room right after supper.

When plans fail, go through each step with the child to see where the breakdown occurred. Fix the specific problem. Remember that a failed plan is not a failure, but an opportunity for success.

## Specific Consequences

The following examples of consequences are drawn from real life. They demonstrate how to develop consequences matched to certain rules.

*The green bag.* We know a parent who warns his children of the green bag, which is coming tomorrow. The next day, the parent puts anything the children have left in the common areas of the house in the green bag. A week later, the green bag is opened. Children are allowed to put the things away. Whatever is not put away is given to a charitable organization.

*The laundry basket.* Another parent we know will only wash what is in the laundry basket. This saves the parent the task of searching for clothes all over the floor. If the child puts only one item in the laundry basket, that one item is all that gets washed.

*The clothes bag.* One child we know refused to get dressed for daycare, although she dressed regularly on Saturday and Sunday. Her mother simply put the child in the car in her pajamas with her clothes in a bag. The child never arrived at daycare in her pajamas. She always changed in the car.

*The jungle room.* The parents of a child with a messy room refused to enter it unless it was clean. They called it the jungle and told the child to keep the door to the jungle closed. They never said the child had to keep the room clean. But when the child wanted a light bulb fixed or something else done in the room, the parents explained that they wouldn't go into the jungle. When the child needed enough help, he cleaned the room.

*The supervised school jaunt.* When one child we know missed the bus because he fussed at home, his mother made him walk. To be sure the child was safe, the mother drove a few yards behind, out of eyeshot, to see that he got to school safely.

Notice in the above examples that by using consequences, parents have less stress and fewer battles with children. Because the consequences are either natural or logical and related to the rule, the person who created the problem (the child) has to solve the problem. Real life is not always as simple as the examples in this chapter. But in the long run, no matter how complex the problems are, they can be solved far more effectively with consequences than with punishments.

# Chapter 6

# Negotiating

Sometimes negotiation is the best way to handle conflict with children. Negotiation is the process of giving and taking through discussion and compromise. It's designed to create a situation where all participants feel they have won, because they get at least some of what they want.

Negotiation is not a sign of weakness, but a sign of strength. It provides children with a model for solving their problems without fighting. Although negotiation can be effective with either big or small problems, it involves a lot of effort. Therefore, it's usually best to reserve negotiation for situations that truly require it.

Negotiation works best when you have reached an impasse with the child because you both legitimately believe you are right. It can also help children resolve their differences with each other.

There are many ways to carry on successful negotiations. They range from quick two-minute exchanges to formal, sit-down, hour-long discussions with a third party acting as mediator. However, all successful negotiations have some elements in common. These are:

- All participants desire a change from the way things are going.

- All participants are willing to listen to each other.

- All participants have equal opportunity to speak within the negotiation.

- All participants understand that equal opportunity does not imply that they have the right to impose their will on the other participants.

- All participants agree in good faith to do their part to make the negotiated solutions work.

- All participants negotiate with the idea of improving the situation, not to seek revenge, exert power or control.

When two people each agree to change a behavior, there is a high rate of failure if the agreement is set up with one person saying if you do..., then I'll do.... For example: In a negotiation, a child agrees to stop teasing her sister if the mother agrees to read a story at bedtime each night.

The problem is that no one is perfect. Sometimes other things occur that cause one person to fail to honor the agreement, even if only once. When that occurs, the other person thinks, You didn't do your part, so why should I do mine?

Then the second person doesn't do what he or she agreed to do. Both people get caught in a downward spiral that is doomed to fail. In the example, Mother has a meeting to go to one evening and can't read a bedtime story. The child gets angry and teases her sister, so the mother refuses to read a story. The whole agreement is dead.

It's better for each person to agree to do his or her part independently of what the other person does. This principle of non-mutuality increases the internal locus of control for everyone. No one's behavior is determined by the behavior of the other.

Set a short time period, a few days perhaps, and then evaluate how well the agreement is working. If one person is doing her or his part, but the other is not, make a new agreement—one with a more realistic chance for success.

## Effective Negotiations

Some resolutions work better than others. The qualities of the most successful resolutions are:

**The agreements are small.** Trying to change too much usually fails. Take on a little at a time.

**The agreements are possible.** Sometimes the participants offer to do more than they are capable of, like reading a story every night when some nights might be spent working. It's better to agree to do something less spectacular but possible to deliver.

**The participants are really willing to do what they agree to do.** They see the benefit of it, even if they ultimately prefer not to do it.

When people compromise, they are agreeing to do something other than what was their first choice. Therefore, there is a built-in reluctance to do what was agreed on. But if they can see a benefit and are genuinely willing to try in good faith, there can be a high degree of success.

*The agreements are set for small periods of time.* The longer the agreement is designed for, the greater the chance for backsliding. A month is probably too long. Try to set up short time periods, and then discuss them again. Reinforce what has worked and try to improve what isn't working.

It often helps to discuss the process of negotiation before the need to use it occurs. A family or class meeting can be held to discuss possible situations for negotiations and how negotiations can be helpful. One possible groundrule is that a negotiation can be called by anyone who needs one.

This agreement provides a forum for at least discussion of the problem among those involved. The negotiation may be between a child and adult, or between two children (with or without adult help), or even between two adults with a child's help, if you so desire.

As we said earlier, negotiation works best when all involved agree to it. However, when you first set up a system for negotiation, strong encouragement might be necessary to get children to participate. If children are listened to and find they receive at least some of what they wanted, they will learn that life is improved by negotiation, at least to some degree. Then not only will children agree to more negotiation, but they will seek it out.

When children request negotiation, we advise you go through with it even if you don't think it is necessary. You may think the reason is not valid or that the child is overusing and abusing the tool. Remember that in the short run, negotiation might seem to be a bother. However, in the long run, you are teaching children to replace fighting, arguing, being stubborn and whining with compromise and negotiation.

# Steps in Negotiating

Let's examine the steps in the negotiation process.

***Each participant takes a turn sharing negative feelings.*** Before it is possible to reach an agreement, it is necessary to clear the air of the negative feelings of the participants. When people are angry, they are more interested in defending their positions or seeking revenge than in seeking workable solutions.

***Each participant takes a turn sharing positive feelings.*** Sometimes it is hard to find something you like about a person at whom you are angry. But by sharing something you appreciate about the other participant, you can reduce tension and get into the frame of mind for working things out.

***Each participant takes a turn making demands.*** The participants state what they want from each other in a clear, precise way.

***The participants negotiate solutions.*** Each participant tells the other what he or she is willing to do to improve the situation.

***The participants reach agreement.*** Each participant agrees to do at least one thing to help resolve the conflict. These agreements are based on the demands and solutions stated above.

***Evaluation responsibilities are determined.*** Evaluation of the agreement helps participants see if the agreement is working. Each person should take a little time to do a modest evaluation. All that is necessary is to tell each other how many times the goal was either met or not met in the given time period.

***The participants set up a time to talk later about how well the agreement is going.*** Once the participants give the agreement a try, it is helpful to get back together in a couple of days to share how well the agreement is going and to fine-tune it if necessary.

*Each participant repeats what the other participants say to ensure understanding.* After each step, it is helpful for each person to paraphrase or repeat what the other has said to be sure the message was accurately heard. Repeating and paraphrasing do not mean agreeing with the statement.

These steps can be modified, reduced or eliminated depending on the time involved, the age of the children and the particular situation.

## Types of Negotiations

Negotiations can be brief or extensive. They can be done only with the people directly involved with the conflict, or with a third or even fourth person. Here are some examples of what negotiations may look like.

—A NEGOTIATION BETWEEN MOTHER AND CHILD—

Notice that some of the steps are streamlined because the daughter is only five years old. Notice also that the mother provides clues and hints for the child.

Mother: Janie, I am really upset that you keep taking stuff out of my purse without asking. I am happy that you usually return it. Do you understand what I'm saying?

Janie: Yes, Mom.

Mother: Do you have anything to say about it? How do you feel when I tell you this?

Janie: I wish I had some makeup that I could play with sometimes.

Mother: Are you happy when I let you play with my old makeup kit?

Janie: Yes, I like it when you give me that kind of stuff.

Mother: I'm willing to buy you some kid's makeup and sometimes let you use my old stuff—if you ask.

Janie: I guess I won't take things out of your purse anymore.

Mother: I can agree to that, but I also want you to ask when you want to use my old makeup. I might not let you use it every time, because it can get messy and I don't always have time to help you clean up.

Janie: OK, I promise to ask.

Mother: OK, I promise to buy you that kid's makeup next weekend.

*Three days later*

Mother: I'm very happy that you haven't gone into my purse, and that yesterday you asked if you could use my old makeup. I'm really glad you didn't throw a tantrum when I said no.

—A VERY QUICK NEGOTIATION BETWEEN A CHILD AND FATHER—

Notice once again how the steps have been shortened and filled in by the father.

Father: I really get angry when you whine when you don't get what you want. Sometimes you accept it and I like that.

Elliot: OK.

Father: You say OK, but I'm not sure you are going to cut down on your whining.

Elliot: I promise.

Father: Is there any way I can help you cut down on your whining? You must understand that when you whine, I get angry. What do you want from me to help you?

Elliot: I don't know. I guess I want you to say yes more often.

Father: You think I don't say yes enough?

Elliot: You hardly ever say yes.

Father: OK. I think I understand. You want me to say yes more often. And I want you to whine less often. I think we can reach an agreement. Want to try?

Elliot: OK.

Father: When you ask for things, I'll either say yes, or at least explain why I say no, so you can understand. And I will never automatically say no, without giving you at least one chance to give me your side. I can't tell you how many times I'll say yes, but I promise that I'll be more open to your ideas. Sometimes, more often than now, I'll give you the green light. How does that sound?

Elliot: Pretty good, I guess.

Father: OK, good. And do you agree to stop whining when I do say no?

Elliot: OK, Dad, I promise.

In this negotiation, the father couldn't promise a set number of yesses, because the child could use that as permission to ask for a number of unfulfillable things, knowing he'd get at least some. The father negotiated honestly and in good faith what he could actually deliver. The father probably knew that he would still say no a number of times, maybe more than his son might like. Conversely, he realized that his son will still whine.

In spite of these limitations, the negotiation achieved the father's goals. It provided a forum for both points of view, gave both the father and his son a chance to say what they wanted, and increased the likelihood that change for the better would occur for both father and son.

—USING A THIRD PARTY—

Notice how in this longer, more formal negotiation, all the steps are followed as described above.

Mom: OK, Jennifer and Danny. You both seem so angry with each other. Want to talk about it?

Jennifer: He took my book and won't give it back.

Danny: Not true. She took my Nintendo game without asking.

Mom: OK. First, Jennifer, tell Danny what he did that's bothering you.

Jennifer: Danny took my book without asking.

Mom: Danny, please tell Jennifer what she is angry about.

Danny: I didn't do anything first.

Mom: Just tell her what she is angry about. It doesn't matter if you agree or not.

Danny: OK. You're mad that I took your book.

Mom: Now, Danny, tell Jennifer what you are angry about.

Danny: She took my game.

Mom: Tell her.

Danny: You took my game.

Mom: Jennifer, tell Danny what he is angry about.

Jennifer: I took his game.

Mom: Tell him.

Jennifer: I took your game.

Mom: Jennifer, now tell Danny one thing he did this week that you like.

Jennifer: That's hard.

Mom: Try hard.

Jennifer: You played with me when my friends weren't around.

Mom: Danny, tell Jennifer what she liked.

Danny: You liked that I played with you.

Mom: Now your turn, Danny. What did you like?

Danny: You helped me pick out a good outfit.

Jennifer: I know, Mom. Danny, you liked that I helped you pick out an outfit.

Mom: Tell Danny what you want him to do.

Jennifer: Don't take my stuff without asking.

Mom: Now you, Danny.

Danny: Don't take my stuff without asking.

Mom: Now you both know what you like and don't like. You both know what you want. What are you willing to do for each other?

Danny: I won't take your stuff without asking.

Jennifer: I won't take your stuff without asking.

Mom: OK, sounds good. Shake hands on it.

(Jennifer and Danny shake hands.)

Mom: Now, lets talk about it in a couple of days and see how it's going.

The third party in the above example was the mother. The third party is used to mediate or help the participants say the most helpful things to each other by following pre-established guidelines. The mediator did not try to enter the negotiation herself, nor did she have a predetermined outcome.

When children are negotiating, a parent, teacher or caregiver can be the mediator. When a parent and child are negotiating, the other parent or another adult, such as a family friend or a grandparent, can be the mediator. Sometimes an older child can mediate. The main requirement is that both of the participants in the negotiation are willing to accept the mediator's directions.

There are many school problems that negotiation can help solve. Direct teacher-student negotiation can be used for such problems as tardiness, incomplete or undone homework, or taking others' belongings without permission. Almost any problem in which either or both teacher and student feel that the other person's behavior is intrusive can be negotiated.

The key question is what is the concrete, tangible negative effect on my life due to the other person's behavior? A statement in response to this question should open the negotiation.

Teachers are often excellent mediators in disputes between classmates. Fighting, cutting in line and name-calling are a few of the problems that have been successfully mediated by teachers. By using the steps in this book and maintaining an attitude of objectivity, many teachers have properly put the locus of control for problem solving back where it belongs—within the student. Negotiation is *not* for moments of crisis when somebody's health or safety is at risk.

# Skills for Mediation

Learning mediation skills is relatively straightforward. The skills can be mastered within a short time. However, using the skills is often difficult. In the heat of battle, emotions can make the mediator forget the neutral, helpful role and get sucked into the conflict. The mediator must take care not to let this happen. The guidelines for the mediator are:

- The mediator is responsible for helping the participants resolve the problem, not resolving it for them.

- The mediator should allow participants time to think and not rush them.

- The mediator should monitor the participants' statements and restrict the use of blame or accusations (e.g., It's your fault).

- The mediator should allow statements of emotion, even if they are said with passion. Statements such as "I hate you when you..." or "I get so angry when..." are difficult to hear, but they help clear the air and pave the way for an agreement.

🕊 The mediator should help the participants recognize and follow the principle of non-mutuality.

Negotiation is a powerful and effective tool. It teaches alternatives to fighting and using power inappropriately to get what you want. Setting up an environment where negotiation is regularly practiced will improve children's communication skills and their ability to get what they want in life.

Negotiation, because it involves compromise, is not always easy for adults or children. However, compromise is often the best alternative.

—THE BATHTUB COURT—

In one family I know, the mediation environment is the bathroom, and it is called "The Bathtub Court." It developed because every time the father was taking a bath, his sons would get into an argument. Finally, the father set up the bathroom court. He acted as judge and jury, while the kids acted as lawyers, prosecutor and defendant.

Each side could make its case, using witnesses when necessary, while the father asked questions. Each side could make one rebuttal to what was presented. When the evidence was given, the father made a judgment that was usually a compromise for both sides.

Using this little drama-game helped the children learn to examine their problems and find peaceful methods for solving them. It used humor and eventually gave the father a little peace in the bathtub.

# Chapter 7

# Humor

When my children were little, I used to play this game with them. They would say, "What would you do if we threw away your newspaper?"

I would answer, "I'd make you go buy me another one, but I'd still love you."

They'd escalate. "What would you do if we threw away your briefcase with your important papers?"

I'd answer, "I'd throw away all of your toys, but I'd still love you."

"What would you do if we threw away your car?"

"I'd ground you for life, use your allowance for life and make you walk to school, but I'd still love you."

Finally, they got as deep as they could get. "What would you do if we threw away the house?"

"I'd take every penny you ever earned for the rest of your lives and make you live in a cardboard box, but I'd still love you."

No matter what they invented to get me angry, I would always end my part with the tag, "I'd still love you." We would all laugh over their creativity in bothering me and my creativity in revenge.

Later, when they really broke a rule, no matter what happened to them, I'd always end with "I still love you." They'd always laugh and take their consequences just a little easier.

Children are often funny. There are many times to laugh at the funny situations they get themselves into. Sometimes you look at the things they do and want to laugh, but are afraid to. You want children to perceive you as serious when you discipline them. But humor can play a significant role in disciplining children.

The benefits of humor are numerous. Studies have shown that laughter prolongs life and plays an important role in preventing disease. Knowing how to laugh at life's problems is a great stress reducer.

Humor can be an important element in relationships. When people are dating, one of the characteristics they most value in their dates is a sense of humor. It's likely that your favorite friends, relatives, teachers, shopkeepers and media personalities have the ability to make you laugh.

# Humor and Discipline

Let's look at some of the roles humor can serve in the area of discipline.

***Humor can defuse power struggles.*** Power struggles occur when you and a child get into a trap, pitting your feeling of dignity against his or hers. The power struggle is rarely based on the original conflict. When power struggles escalate, they can only get worse. The only way for either party to feel that they have not lost the struggle is to save face.

It is very difficult, in the heat of battle, to understand the real issues. Humor can take the pressure off and provide a chance for both parties to cool off. It is difficult to hold onto anger while you are smiling.

—BIKES AND BABOONS—

> You and a child are fighting over putting a bike away. The child keeps saying no, and you keep saying do it! Just as you are ready to nail the child to the wall, you say, "Don't we sound like a couple of babbling baboons? I bet if we were at the zoo right now, we'd be locked in the monkey house."

***We can encourage the child not to take problems so seriously.*** Because problems seem to increase in severity as we get older, it is often difficult for adults to take children's problems seriously. A child can be just as upset by not being able to find a toy as an adult can be about not being able to find the car keys. A child feels just as bad about missing a favorite television show as you do when you miss your exercise class or a playoff game.

Yet problems often have a lighter side. Distance usually allows us the luxury of laughing at a situation that once made us cry. When we help children find humor in problem situations without trivializing their pain, we give them a skill that will make their entire life more pleasurable.

—PLANE CRASH—

A child breaks a model plane and is whining and fussing endlessly. After you show that you are truly sorry, you say, "We better get Congress to buy another jet before the president finds out this one is missing. I think it was his favorite." Perhaps you can help the child write a budget amendment for a new model, and go together to buy one.

***Humor allows us to be genuine.*** When we stifle our desire to laugh when our kids are funny because we want to appear stern and firm, we hide our true feelings. Children are very adept at seeing when we are genuine and when we are not. In the long run, it is better to be the way we are than to pretend to be different.

—THE MISPLACED MEAL—

Your daughter dumps her food on the floor and gets it all over her lap. The scene is funny. She looks at you, wondering what you will do. Instead of shouting and yelling, you simply laugh at how funny she looks.

***Humor enhances relationships.*** Humor brings people closer. People who laugh together solve differences faster. Families that laugh together are less susceptible to breaking apart. Games like the "I'd still love you" one described earlier illustrate the use of humor in this way.

***Humor reduces stress.*** Humor is a natural stress reducer. For example, a child is tense about missing a homework assignment, and you tell him or her a funny story about a time when you missed an assignment.

***Humor can be used to defuse tension.*** Humor can sometimes act like a vaccine. It can stop a potential power struggle before it begins.

—BAIT AND SWITCH—

A child puts out the bait for you to fall into a power struggle. Before responding to the bait, you say, "It sounds like you are looking for me to argue with you, but I'm either too old or too slow to fight today. Why don't you come back tomorrow when I'm younger and faster?"

***Humor can diminish tension, so another consequence can be used effectively.*** Sometimes we use threats and scoldings when we don't want to. Because our feelings are hot, we lose the strength to avoid attacking the dignity and self-esteem of the child. As tension rises between the adult and child, we are unlikely to change the kid's behavior in a positive way. Humor can ease the tension so we can replace the punishment with a consequence.

For example, you lose control and give the child one of those scolding, you-better-shape-up-or-else lectures. He or she responds with anger and resistance. You feel the urge to get tougher, but you are smart enough to realize that neither you nor the child can win if you do. Instead, use humor to deflate the tension. Then replace the lecture with a consequence that will work.

***Humor can be used as a mirror.*** Humor can be used to show the child what he or she looks like when he or she behaves in a certain way. By laughing at the behavior, the child can see potentially dangerous choices in a non-threatening way, what the results might be and how to change. This technique must be done with care to ensure that it doesn't revert to mocking or ridiculing the child.

When a child is whining, you can say as straightforwardly and non-sarcastically as possible, "That's pretty good whining. Mind if I join in?" Then you whine together.

—THE RIOT ACT—

Here's an example of a serious problem that was solved more with humor than anything else. My son was caught lighting matches. Part of his dresser was burned. After his mother read him the riot act, I was called in to follow through with riot act II.

I found him lying in bed, overcome with fear and guilt. He was in no shape to plan a solution to his problem. I sat with him and told him that I had done the same thing when I was his age and I got caught, too. We laughed at how similar the lectures we received were.

I told him what I was supposed to be saying. "You know, this is serious, and I should be saying, 'If I ever catch you playing with matches again, I'll give it to you but good. You know how dangerous this is. You can burn down the whole house.'" I went on with mock crazed anger.

Once he laughed, I gave him a hug and said, "This is serious, you know." He said that he knew. Then we were able to talk about it calmly, without fear and guilt, and find a way to stop the behavior. Not only did the behavior cease, but we never felt closer.

## Potential Dangers

In spite of the many positive uses for humor in discipline situations, there are potential dangers in its misuse. Let's look at some of the possible dangers and examine ways to avoid them.

*The possibility that children won't take you seriously when you are disciplining them.* Making a joke about breaking a rule might give children the false impression that you aren't serious about disciplining them. This danger is increased if you frequently laugh at misbehavior. Children can soon learn that naughty is cute and breaking rules is funny.

*Giving mixed messages.* If sometimes a parent or teacher is firm and other times funny, children might become confused and not know what to expect. The ability to predict an outcome is lessened, and it becomes more difficult for the child to control his or her own behavior.

*Losing control of the situation.* If laughing at the situation encourages more negative behavior, the chance to stop the behavior might be delayed or lost.

*The fear that the child might get away with something or the fear that the child might think you are condoning an undesired behavior.* Both of these fears relate to believing that laughter might let the child think he or she can do whatever he wants as long as he or she can make you laugh.

All of these fears are valid. Whether they are realized depends on many factors. If you are usually firm with children and fair in dealing with them, a little humor will not destroy how serious you are in disciplining them.

Humor should not replace natural and logical consequences. Humor should not be used to tell children that they are cute when doing something that is unacceptable or harmful to others.

However, humor can reduce tension and anger and provide an environment in which an ineffective consequence can be replaced with an effective one. Humor can open doors to reach new levels of a positive relationship. Humor can heal wounds.

Good humor is a wonderful way to display your warm, human side. When used with care, it can lighten potentially heavy situations and make life more pleasant and more worth living.

# Chapter 8

# The Bottom Line

We have suggested in this book the importance of telling and showing children what you want. We have described how to create good rules and consequences, how to negotiate and how to help kids feel in control of themselves. In this chapter, we wish to make the important point that children sometimes need our firm and unwavering guidance so that we may help them achieve their fullest potential.

We need to communicate high standards and expectations to children. We do not negotiate with an 18 month old about whether to drink the Drano that is under the sink. We say no. We may hope that eventually our no is enough, but until it is, we move the Drano to an inaccessible place.

Putting safety plugs into outlets, erecting barriers with gates or other furniture, ensuring that a teenager has a driver's license before giving him or her the car keys are some common behaviors that aren't usually thought of as discipline. However, in each instance we are communicating our expectations—and furthermore, insisting on compliance—even by rearranging the house if necessary.

The same principle of setting a bottom line with less obvious but still potentially harmful behaviors is important during the formative years. Throughout a child's development, you want to involve her or him as much as possible when it comes to decisions and choices that affect her or his life.

The early years of childhood are the prime years in the child's development of conscience and morality. Before children can make choices well, they need to know which behaviors gain approval and disapproval from parents and important others.

Young children do not yet reason well, so they are especially dependent on the feedback their behavior gets from those who love and care for them. When children hear and feel approval through smiles, applause and hugs, they get encouragement to continue their behavior. A firm verbal and nonverbal no offers the opposite feedback.

Paul Tournier, in *To Resist or Surrender*, writes, "There are many parents who do not want to argue with their children over every mistake. They reserve their authority for serious matters, but then it is too late. By forever giving in they lose all authority."

## Be Firm, Clear and Specific

The time to be firm, clear and specific is when children are young. Enjoying children is wonderful and necessary, but enjoyment without limits during the early years will lead to spoiled, indulged older children and adolescents.

Parents, teachers and caregivers need to intervene the first time a child bites, pulls hair, pinches, throws food, hits another child, doesn't do homework or swears. The child needs to hear from us in a firm, no-nonsense manner.

The child needs to be quickly shown better, less harmful alternatives. If limits and controls are lacking in the early years, children will be at a loss for proper behavior later on and will also be more likely to rebel against any kind of authority.

During early childhood, children need to learn appropriate social graces. These include the following skills:

- Don't interrupt when others are talking.
- Say please and thank you.
- Cover your mouth when coughing or sneezing.
- Say excuse me.
- Apologize.
- Wait your turn.
- Remain quiet in certain situations (school, church, etc.).
- Answer the phone politely.
- Return borrowed items without reminders and on time.

ᴥ Write a thank-you note or make an appreciative phone call when gifts are received.

These expectations further a child's developing sense of responsibility.

The early years provide caring adults with many opportunities to teach children important life skills that lead to self-discipline. During these early years, your behavior as a parent, teacher or caregiver makes a much more powerful impact than your words.

# Setting Effective Limits

Setting bottom lines for children requires us to set and follow bottom lines for ourselves. We should model in our lives what we want children to do in theirs. The old proverbial adage reminds us that the apple rarely falls far from the tree.

As adults, we need to be aware of how we solve problems and what that teaches children. A parent who instructs a child to tell callers that the parent isn't home sends child the message that it is OK to lie. Teachers who publicly criticize and humiliate students teach that performance is more important than self-esteem. Parents who don't set clear limits around homework, chores at home or practicing a skill until mastery is gained are telling their children that self-discipline is unimportant to success.

Parents who volunteer their time to help others teach the value of sharing. Teachers who emphasize the positive are telling kids that they are special. These lessons are much more powerful than the words we use.

Establishing bottom lines is really not very difficult, especially when begun early. It is okay to firmly say no when an objectionable behavior occurs. If food is thrown on the floor, the child is told food is not for throwing. It needs to be picked up now. A child who is banging on furniture is told that tables are not for banging.

Should the behavior continue, a clearer repetition of the message is given. If the child still does not comply, the child's hands are held, or he or she is offered a few minutes of timeout. If screaming accompanies the timeout or the hands being held, you say, "You're really unhappy now, but tables (people, etc.) are not for banging."

Following a few such messages, most children get the message and learn the importance of showing appropriate respect for people and property. We offer these additional suggestions for setting effective limits or bottom lines that help children become more responsible.

*Give children regular work responsibilities.* This concept has been discussed earlier, but we mention it again because of its importance. Children who have regular work responsibilities develop a feeling of healthy achievement and a sense of community—I'm a part of something more than just me.

*Expect caring, sensitive behavior from children.* It is never too early to begin teaching children how to show caring, respect and sensitivity toward other people. Rude behavior should be dealt with in a caring but firm way as soon as it is seen.

If a child pokes fun at someone else, we need to quickly show the child how hurtful that can be. When a child is being a bully, then we need both to show more attention to the child and to deal firmly with the behavior.

Tell the child, "You will not hit other children." Look the child squarely in the eye and express this with an unmistakable I-mean-business quality. These actions communicate strongly your respect for the rights of others. Follow up with a choosing or planning question (see Chapters 4 and 5).

*Encourage and expect that children finish what they start.* Not all tasks are fun, nor can all tasks be completed quickly. Yet there is much value in learning self-discipline at an early age. Some jobs are best left quickly, especially if they are too difficult, frustrating or even dangerous. But providing strong guidance and encouragement around most children's pursuits pays dividends in the long haul.

The main difference between successful and less successful children and adults is in their persistence. Reward children's efforts. Set aside a study or quiet time in which reading, homework or practicing music is the only acceptable activity. As with all the other suggestions, the earlier one begins, the more likely the child is to develop good habits.

***Do not rescue children.*** Allow children to learn through natural and logical consequences what the results of their effort or lack of effort are. Parents should allow children to incur the teacher's disapproval for an incomplete assignment, rather than writing an excuse.

Children learn responsibility by being given it and by being held accountable for their actions. Develop good consequences that teach children the value of more responsible behavior.

Behavior changes slowly and often gets worse before it gets better. Children will not give up whining, throwing tantrums, kicking or screaming easily, especially when those behaviors have worked for them in the past. Giving in may seem easier than holding firm. You will need to be a good limit setter as well as an active listener.

Teachers and caregivers also must develop the skill of setting limits. Children can know that you understand how they feel, but that you won't continue to do things that will be harmful in the long run. Just as changing difficult habits such as smoking and losing weight can be frustrating at times, so too can be the process of helping children learn or relearn the value of patience, work and responsibility.

***Take other people's feedback seriously.*** It is natural for parents to want to defend and side with their children when others outside the family express concerns about behavior. This is often true of teachers as well. It is natural to want to defend and side with the children in our own class. We often think of them as "our kids." When our kids get into trouble, we first want to believe that it must be the fault of the strict teacher on yard duty, the bad influence of another child or a stage the kids are going through.

While any or all of these things may be true, the fact is that you have been notified about a concern that someone else has about a child. It is important to discuss this feedback with the child.

Feedback helps the child see how he or she might have contributed to what happened. This discussion can also help you understand why there is a problem. Once you see the picture, you might work with the child to develop a plan for more appropriate behavior in such situations.

***Confront calmly with actions and few words.*** We have offered many techniques to use when you want to change a child's behavior. They include I-statements, listening skills, planning skills, the broken record technique, problem-solving meetings and discussion.

However, when none of these have worked to change the behavior, it will probably be necessary to stop doing things for the child. Then she or he will experience the natural consequences of her or his refusal to be a responsible member of the family or class.

Parents can refuse to cook dinner, wash clothes or be the morning alarm clock, be unavailable to drive a child to a friend's house, etc. These choices tell the child that cooperation is a necessity and works both ways.

Parents must be careful to take these actions matter-of-factly, with respect for the child and without sarcasm. Otherwise, a power struggle and more conflict in the relationship is likely to result. When the child demands clean clothes, the parent politely states, "I do laundry only for those in the family who do their jobs."

It should rarely be necessary to get to such a point with children, especially when they have learned and experienced the value of natural consequences, when there has been the development of good communication between a caring adult and a child and when there has been a spirit of cooperation through problem solving to settle disputes rather than an insistence on do it my way or else.

The main purpose of the kind of confrontation discussed here is to open the door when difficult problems exist, so a real plan can be developed by the adult and child for more responsible behavior in the future.

# Chapter 9

# Family Living

Families today have little in common with the family depicted in the oldies television show "Father Knows Best." If that show was aired today, it might have to be retitled "Where Has Father Gone?"

## Family Structures

There are many structures that describe a family. There are structures with two parents, one working; two parents, both working; single parents, either mother or father; parent and grandparent families, with one or both working; families with unmarried parent substitutes; and blended families. It is difficult, if not impossible, to define a norm. No one definition fits more than 50 percent of all U.S. families. Each family type has its own strengths.

Many single parents and children have lived most of their lives together without even knowing any other kind of family, except on television. The term *latch-key children* once was used by a few professionals. It is now a common household word. At one time, children of divorced parents hid their family status and were ashamed of it. Now children of divorced parents are so common that they do not think it is even worth talking about.

Each family has certain unique challenges when it comes to discipline. Let's examine the more common family types and explore how structure affects discipline.

***Two parents, one at home.*** This is the closest current example to the ideal family of the '50s. However, the parent at home may be either the father or mother. Some families alternate who is at home.

In relation to discipline, the strengths of this family structure include having a parent always at home to deal with problems, to spend time with children, to teach family values and to provide long-term continuity. This family also has the strength of two parents to back up policies, to discuss difficult decisions and make wise choices, and to give the children more than one role model.

However, there are problems within this seemingly ideal structure.

- Sometimes parents disagree on the best way to discipline children. These disagreements can be very powerful and sometimes create major family problems. Because raising children is related to the central values of each parent, compromise can be very difficult.

- Sometimes the children play one parent off the other. Even when there is only minor disagreement, children quickly learn who is the soft touch and who to avoid when they want something.

- Sometimes the parents' problems with each other rub off on the children. When parents argue about issues unrelated to the children, they may take it out on the children.

- One parent may feel that he or she takes on more of the parenting role than the other. Usually, the parent at home feels this way.

Each of these problems can be minimized through effective communication. Regularly scheduled family meetings help a great deal, and informal discussions are useful. Don't wait for a problem to develop to discuss what you think is important about discipline.

Agree on the rules and consequences together. Don't let children play one parent against the other. While a totally united front may sound great, it is often difficult to achieve and may leave children feeling overwhelmed and powerless. Open discussions with give-and-take on everyone's part may be more effective in the long run.

Parents can read this and other books together. Discuss your reading over dessert or during a dinner alone. Share honest opinions about the pros and cons of many different ideas.

You do not need to convince your spouse that you are right. Simply try to understand each other's point of view and come to a mutual agreement on the major issues. Remember that agreements can be modified and renegotiated.

**Two parents, both work.** The main difference between this family and the one described earlier is that the children probably spend more time in daycare. Therefore, they learn a different discipline system that may or may not specifically reflect the values of the family.

In addition, each parent is equally tired after work, and both parents want to come home to a trouble-free environment. When discipline problems await, patience is strained.

Families with two working parents must work harder to find time to do things together. Discipline issues seem magnified because of the limited time together and the demands of competing needs and pressures.

These families need a sense of perspective. It's harder to think of discipline as a learning opportunity, and greater patience is required. It is important to find time for pleasurable family activities, even short ones, nearly every day. Discipline challenges can be more easily handled when time has been spent in shared activities.

***Single parent families.*** Single parent families avoid the problem of disagreements and differing points of view. The parent in charge makes the decisions and that's that. The child must deal with that parent, because no one else is there to play against that parent.

Single parent families often have great strength, because the children and parent need each other and because survival of the family is typically more threatened. Under these instances, the family becomes insular and protective.

The main problem of discipline in single parent families is related to intensity. Because there is only one adult in the house, everything must be done by that parent. There is no one with whom to discuss and process the daily discipline challenges. Friends and other family members can listen and offer suggestions, but they are not on the front line as another parent would be. There is no one to take over and give the single parent a break.

From the children's point of view, if they are having a bad time with their parent, they have no one else to turn to. When they get angry they risk alienating the only caregiver. They have no cooler head to appeal to when things get tense.

Aside from remarriage, there are few options to change these realities. Single parents can learn to manage their stress and to teach their children to handle theirs.

It is often difficult for the single parent not to feel guilty about taking care of his or her own needs and desires. More care must be taken by single parents to meet their own needs for being alone and to take time to be an adult without children to care for. Give yourself at least an hour every day to read or take a hot bath or to do anything that makes you feel good about the adult part of you.

Care must be taken not to feel angry or guilty about your situation. Simply accept your home as your reality and make the best decisions you can. We hope some of the suggestions in this book can give you the extra guidance you are missing without an additional adult in the home.

Build on the unique and special qualities that bring single parents and their children close. Do things with your kids that are fun for both of you. Make meals together. Give the children a small budget to buy what they want to eat, and shop together.

Finally, learn to trust your instincts. If you are the only adult making discipline decisions, give yourself permission to do what you think is right. It is OK to make mistakes. Learn from them. Use some of the guidelines in this book to review how you are dealing with your children. You can improve your discipline skills as your children learn to improve their behavior.

**Blended families.** Blended families are rich in experience and family culture. They provide opportunities for new sibling relationships and sharing of new interests. The problems related to blended families have to do with defining roles, the built-in tendency to compete for attention, and jealousies.

When men suddenly become fathers and women suddenly become mothers, they can be reluctant to believe their role as parents is real, even though the desire to be a new parent is genuine. But the new parent may feel unsure of how much authority to take and how the children and the new spouse will accept that authority. Being the new kid on the block always requires an adjustment period.

To help this transition go smoothly, the natural parent can give the new parent full freedom to be a real parent. Back the new parent up when he or she takes a stand, and encourage him or her to step in whenever he or she wants.

As we have suggested many times before, discipline does not start with rule violations. It begins with family activities. The new parent needs to interact with the children by reading bedtime stories, playing games, listening to problems, being the one to bandage a minor wound and helping with homework. The children might be reluctant to accept the new parent, but with patience and gentle perseverance, this reluctance will fade.

It is important in blended families for the people with problems to speak to each other, rather than about each other to the parent in the middle. If you are the natural parent, do not get into the trap of allowing either the child or your spouse to complain to you about the other. You can never win by accepting this responsibility, and your family will never normalize.

Another potential problem with blended families occurs when two sets of children come together. Rivalries and jealousy can emerge when children believe that other children are getting more attention than they are. Children may act out and show their anger in passive-aggressive ways. The result is added tension for everyone and escalating discipline problems.

Family meetings can help ease tensions and provide a healthy outlet for built-up resentments. At other times, listen to children's complaints without minimizing their validity. If children indicate, by their words or actions, that you are not giving them enough attention, recognize that in their eyes, an injustice is being done to them.

While explanations of your point of view are necessary, they are not sufficient to solve the problem. Ask the children what they need, and give them at least some of what they want.

Sometimes blended families can find creative solutions to unusual problems. For example: A Jewish man with children joined a Christian woman with children. The man grew up believing that Christmas trees do not belong in Jewish homes. The woman always had a Christmas tree. After many go-rounds about the way their new household should be, they decided to designate one room as the Hanukkah room and another room as the Christmas room.

Both felt comfortable with this solution, and the children not only got a first-hand look at a new culture, they also saw creative problem solving, negotiation and compromise modeled in their home. They saw that two people can both win even when they have different and strongly held views.

## Coping with Stress

Throughout this book, we have emphasized how important it is that children develop a positive sense of self, high self-esteem. Children's self-esteem is developed as they learn strategies that help them cope with their complex world. Children need to learn that it is OK to smile at themselves and to feel good about who they are.

Children can show significant symptoms of stress as early as preschool. The fast-paced, never-ending array of competing choices and demands can lead to substantial stress even among children who have strong supportive families. Childhood discipline problems can often be related to stress.

As a very important person in the lives of children, you have opportunities to teach children effective ways to deal with stress. The following relaxation methods can be used by children or adults.

***Get exercise.*** A one-, two- or three-mile walk each day can do wonders for alleviating unwanted stress. Some people prefer aerobic exercise, while others like to run. Whatever it is, try to choose an exercise that has little, if any, competition.

We know some executives who play racquetball during their lunch hour. They often return to the office more stressed-out than when they left, because they attach too much importance to winning and losing.

***Use mind-calming exercises.*** Sit back in a comfortable chair for a few moments and try one or more of the following exercises:

- Count to five with your eyes closed as you breathe in. Then hold your breath for a count of five. Then breathe out as you silently count to five. Do this for a few moments.

- Do the same breathing exercise, but picture yourself breathing in healthy, relaxed air as you breathe in to your count of five. When you breathe out, picture all the stress and tension leaving your body in the exhaled breath.

- Breathe in and silently say the word *calm*. Breathe out while you silently say *down*. Do this several times, repeating *calm—down*. You might even hear yourself silently saying *calm, calm, calm, calm* (a few or even several times) as you breathe in, and *down, down, down, down* (also a few or several times) as you breathe out. As with the earlier exercises, doing this with eyes closed in an environment relatively free of distractions for a few minutes can be very helpful.

- Take yourself to a relaxing movie in your own mind. Close your eyes and take yourself to the beach, the mountains or to a favored place that you have actually visited. Picture yourself in this setting.

  If it is the beach, actually see yourself lying on the sand, hearing the ocean waves lapping ashore as the sun enters each and every pore of your body, soaking through the tension and replacing it with calm relaxation.

  When you have a clear picture of what you are seeing, allow yourself to enter the picture. Step into the screen and actually be there for a few moments. Enjoy the peace, quietness and relaxation. Bring these feelings back with you to work, to home or to wherever you have to be next.

&#x25aa; Before exploding at someone or saying something that you know will hurt, pause, count to ten and then ask yourself what you want to do next.

*Use body-relaxing methods.* When the tension remains and you just can't seem to let it go, it can sometimes help to squeeze a pillow or towel, bite a pillow or towel or even scream into a pillow. Sometimes doing a combination of these can temporarily alleviate the tension.

Close your eyes and find a relaxing position. You are going to squeeze the tension out of your body. Begin at your toes. Scrunch up your toes for five seconds and then release. Do it again (scrunch up your toes and release). Feel the relaxation as you release. Now do the same thing to other parts of your body, working your way up from toes to head. (Omit areas that have medical problems.)

We suggest focusing on your ankles, calves, thighs, buttocks, tummy, chest, shoulders, arms, fingers, neck, head and face. When you feel relaxed, you might want to do one or more of the mind-calming exercises.

*Try to find a solution to the problem.* You might find the steps listed in the problem-solving chapter (Chapter 10) helpful when you are dealing with someone who is giving you a hard time. You might want to talk problems over with a trusted friend.

If you do not have close friends, that may in itself be stressful. Men in particular are often very lonely. Few men have intimate, trusted friends. You may need to reach out more. Join a health club or an awareness group.

Regardless of what your family structure is, you will face discipline problems that are unique to you and your children. The basic skills and principles in this book are universal. By understanding the unique strengths and discipline concerns of your family, you can be all the more effective in preventing problems and in dealing with them when they occur.

# Chapter 10

# Solving Problems Together

Learning to make decisions requires opportunities and practice. The family or classroom becomes alive and exciting when children's problems or problems among family members are greeted as an opportunity to practice and refine decision-making and problem-solving skills.

We must trust that with a little help from us, children have it within themselves to find solutions to problems. The ideas and activities in this chapter provide ways of building cooperative bonds between caring adults and children enabling them to work together to solve problems.

While some activities are more family oriented, the process explained can be applied to classroom situations. The family council explained below could become a classroom council with a few modifications.

# Family Council

We have found that weekly family council meetings with all family members present for 30 minutes to an hour can be a very useful structure in which problems can be identified and possible solutions offered. It is also a time when daily or weekly highlights (good things that have happened or good deeds done for others) can be shared. The following suggestions can help you plan and organize a family council meeting.

*Share appreciation.* A good way to begin such meetings is to have each family member share one or two positive experiences that have happened since the last meeting. This enables all family members to keep in touch with each other, which can be difficult with all the competing demands in the lives of both children and adults.

Sharing appreciations provides a tone of support in which later problem solving can occur.

*List concerns or problems.* The leader of the council (generally Mother or Father, although this responsibility can be shared on a rotating basis) makes a list of concerns or problems that any or all members want to discuss. To get a list started, the leader asks: "Are there any problems any of us have that we can work together on solving today?"

—SOME POSSIBLE PROBLEMS—

Ted keeps walking into my room without knocking.

I think it is unfair that I do all of the chores and nobody else around here does their share.

I am concerned, Sue, that your teacher called twice about your homework not getting done. Maybe all of us can put our heads together to figure this out.

Joey keeps stealing my toys. Then he hits me when I try to get them back.

**Discuss problems.** Decide which problems are most appropriate for solving in family council and which ones are best addressed at another time or in a different setting. When a problem is chosen for discussion, all family members present are encouraged to share their ideas.

Before the meeting ends, each problem should either have been discussed and solved or an alternative plan developed that notes when or how the problem will get solved. The alternative plan may simply state that more work needs to be done.

—AN ALTERNATIVE PLAN—

Sue doesn't want to discuss her homework woes with everybody there. She and Mom agree to meet separately.

**Summarize decisions.** The solutions and work to be done are summarized at the end.

—A SUMMARY—

So, Joey, you agree to not take Bob's toys when he is playing with them. Bob, in case he does take your toys and you want them back, you'll first tell him. If that doesn't work, you'll tell Mom or Dad.

***Plan for the future.*** Finally, each family member who has had a problem solved should state in his or her own words what he or she is going to do in the future.

# Steps of Problem Solving

Involving children as problem solvers sends a strong message of respect. You are really saying you believe in their ability to actively participate in a meaningful way to help solve problems and make this a better place. It is one of the best ways that you can communicate trust and build self-esteem.

There are many methods to use in solving problems. You should do what is most comfortable and natural for you, while realizing that good discipline through problem solving takes time and practice for both adults and children.

The skills required to do problem solving with children are good listening, a clear and nonblaming way of telling the child your own thoughts and feelings and trust and belief that the child can, with assistance, make good decisions. In the book *How to Talk So Kids Will Listen and How to Listen So Kids Will Talk* (Faber and Mazlish, 1982), the authors describe a problem-solving method that can be of help to children and caregivers.

***Talk about the child's feelings and needs.*** (It's probably annoying when I ask you to pick up your toys and put them away before you go out to play.)

***Listen to what the child says.*** Listen until the child seems finished expressing her or his feelings. Do not underestimate the value and meaning of good listening. Children need to know that their thoughts, feelings and ideas are valued even if you disagree with their point of view.

***Talk about your feelings and needs.*** (On the other hand, when toys are left on the floor, people could trip over them and hurt themselves. So if you leave your toys lying around, that creates more work for me.)

***Brainstorm to find a mutually agreeable solution.*** (Let's put our heads together and come up with some ideas that would be good for us.)

***Write down all the ideas.*** Don't evaluate them at this point. You are trying to come up with as many solutions as you can without concern about which ones are good and which ones are not.

—A Brainstorming List—

In the case of toys on the floor, some of the ideas might include:

I could give up playing with my friends.

Throw out toys that are left on the floor.

Put toys left on floor in a big bag in the basement. Give the toys left in the bag after one week to the Salvation Army.

Keep toys lying around. Use allowance to pay doctor bill for any injury that someone gets by tripping on them.

Make sure I pick up toys before going out.

Give a reminder that toys need to be picked up if child forgets.

***Choose a solution.*** Together, you and the child decide which solutions are likely to solve the problem and which probably won't. (Mom and child decide that the best solutions are that a reminder be given that toys need to get picked up. If they are not picked up they will be placed in a big bag. Toys that are unclaimed within a week will be given to a local charity.)

It takes wisdom to know when to get involved in solving problems with children, when to solve problems for children, and when to allow children to solve their own problems.

All children will eventually have problems. Brothers, sisters or other children will hit or tease. Children will sooner or later have difficulty with a teacher. Whether living in a tough neighborhood or not, most children will eventually be threatened or bullied. It is just a matter of time until kids feel peer pressure, including pressure to take drugs or have sex.

We can best prepare children to deal with these eventualities by teaching them at early ages how to identify problems and how to solve them. Children need to believe that there are few, if any, problems that can't be solved.

Sometimes the best outcome is that children find someone who cares about them to talk to while experiencing stress. But often there are specific strategies that a child can take to solve a problem. From about the age of four on, when children experience problems they can verbalize, we can lead them through specific steps so that ultimately they learn to solve problems on their own. These steps are as follows:

**Ask what the problem is.** Say the problem out loud or say it quietly to yourself. This helps children to get clear about the problem.

**Consider the possibilities.** Jermaine is in the schoolyard when three kids (out of view of the teacher) grab the hat from his head and start tossing it back and forth. Jermaine has learned that there are four basic ways to solve problems: (1) fight my way out, (2) talk my way out, (3) run my way out, or (4) get someone else to help me out. He needs to decide which way is best.

**Develop a plan.** Before Jermaine can know which of these possibilities is best for him in this difficult situation, he must ask himself several questions quickly. How tough am I? How tough are they? Are there other kids looking on? If so, how can I save face and also not get my face busted up? Are there other people around to help me? Can I get them to help me without being thought of as a wimp? What kinds of words can I use that might get me out of this?

He reminds himself that talking, running or asking for help is better than fighting. Even if you are tougher, you can never be sure about things like weapons. But he doesn't want to back down, because other kids are looking on and he doesn't want to be seen as a weak target in the future.

He decides on a plan. He'll ask for his hat back. If they don't give it back, he'll tell them he wants it back later and walk away rather than fight. He figures three against one is unfair and getting hurt over a hat isn't worth it.

**Use the plan.** Jermaine says to the bullies, "Hey, it's cold! Please give me back my hat." Not only do they not give him the hat back, but they laugh and make it obvious that he'll have to challenge them if he wants it back.

Jermaine, remembering that a hat isn't worth a bloody face, says, "I can see that you really want to play with my hat. I'd like it back when you are through with it." Jermaine walks away.

**Decide if the plan worked.** Jermaine's plan really involved three different problems: getting his hat back, not getting beat up, saving face in front of other kids. He eventually got his hat back (even though it was wet and muddy). He realizes that he didn't get beaten up and his friends are still friends, especially because he knew a really good thing to say when he was outnumbered.

Jermaine decides that his plan was effective. If it was not effective, then it would be time for him to backtrack and once again go through the steps. To review, these are:

- Ask what the problem is.
- Consider the possibilities.
- Develop a plan.
- Use the plan.
- Decide if the plan worked.

# Using the Group

Teachers, youth leaders and others who work in groups with children can often use the group effectively to solve problems, especially when their efforts haven't worked. Let's take a situation where one child is being picked on by several other children.

A leader can use the following procedure in such instances:

Be sure the child who has been picked on is not present. Ask the other children the following question: How do you feel about (the child)'s behavior? This gives the children an opportunity to express their feelings before doing the problem solving.

Ask: Why do·you think (the child) acts this way? or How do you think he or she feels inside? With younger children, ask: Do you think (the child) likes or doesn't like her- or himself?

Ask: What do you think you could do besides just hating (the child)?

In such a situation, what usually occurs is that the child being picked on has low self-esteem and actually does many things to irritate others. The child sees the negative attention as better than none at all, which is what the victim he or she believes would happen if he or she acted in some other way.

The other children, feeling irritated, pick on the victim, thereby continuing the cycle. We have found that once the other children are aware of how the victim feels and what motivates that behavior, they are often willing to become part of the solution to the problem.

Solving problems is a skill that can be learned and practiced by both adults and children. This skill is essential in all relationships with other people—adult-adult, adult-child or child-child. Helping children learn and practice problem-solving skills empowers them to find solutions for themselves and others.

# Chapter 11

# Common Problems, Situations and Solutions

In this chapter we discuss many common and difficult problems that caring adults face in teaching, tending and raising children. We share a number of possible solutions for each problem.

## Tantrums and Other Common Problems

Temper tantrums are a common problem that all parents face sooner or later. Teachers and caregivers face them as well. It really does not matter how calm or gentle a person you are. Outbursts can be frustrating, frightening and upsetting, especially if you aren't prepared to understand that all children will have them and that you are not a bad parent, teacher or caregiver because they do.

Basically, a temper tantrum is an immature way of expressing anger. The challenge is to teach children that anger is okay and that there are better ways to express this emotion. Children need to learn that temper tantrums will not get them what they want or change your mind.

Most children with a history of severe tantrums have learned that tantrums can be an extremely effective way to get what they want. They quickly learn that caring adults don't like to see a child upset and suffering. They discover that when they want either to avoid a responsibility or to get something that is at first denied, a tantrum will make an adult feel guilty and embarrassed (especially if it's done in public).

In this book, we have shared many ways to teach children to express their feelings effectively and appropriately. By two or three years of age, most children can learn to verbalize their feelings. It is important that you teach them how to do so. Active listening (you feel angry because...) provides a good outlet for anger. If you start doing this when a child is young, tantrums will rarely last beyond the preschool years.

There are different reasons for temper tantrums. Try to figure out why a child is having a tantrum. There are five different types of tantrums described by Dr. Barton Schmitt (1987).

***Frustration tantrums.*** These occur when a child is trying to master something and is having a hard time. The best response to this type of tantrum is to offer encouragement and to say something brief that shows understanding.

—I Understand—

I can see how hard that is for you and how hard you are trying. I know you'll get better at it. Is there something that I can do to help? (An arm around the shoulder can work wonders while you are sharing this moment of compassion.)

***Demanding tantrums.*** These occur when the child wants something and his or her path is blocked. Toy stores and supermarkets are common locations for this type of tantrum.

—The Toy Truck—

Matt sees that toy truck and starts working on you. You try to distract him, but he's persistent. His request quickly turns to whining, which if unsuccessful, can lead to a full-blown tantrum.

Naturally, you become embarrassed, afraid your neighbors or fellow workers are in the store shopping and will see that you are unable to control your child. You either give in and buy the truck, or promise Matt that if he stops, you'll get it for him next time. Matt has won!

It is best to ignore these types of tantrums. Reflect the desire (I know you want that truck), but quickly set a no-nonsense limit (but today we are here only for the game). When Matt begins to whine, tell him that he can either stop or you'll leave the store. If he doesn't stop, then leave.

***Attention tantrums.*** These tantrums often occur while you are attempting to have a phone conversation, when you're in the shower, when you have just sat down to read the newspaper or perhaps even as you enter the bathroom. These tantrums are also most likely to occur on rainy, miserable days when everybody's temper is a tad short.

The best way to deal with these is to offer as little attention as possible. Move away from the child—escape if necessary to a different room. Tell the child that you can only listen when she or he is able to talk like a big girl or boy. Children with frequent or severe attention-seeking tantrums generally need positive, perhaps more frequent contact from you that feels satisfying.

—PHYLLIS NEEDS ATTENTION—

A nine-year-old girl's single mother recently asked for advice, because this normally responsible child had been having increased episodes of tantrums over the past several months. They were progressively getting worse.

As I talked with the child, Phyllis, she confided that her four-year-old sister with cerebral palsy, who was dependent for feeding and toileting, was getting all the attention. Phyllis was mad about it.

Phyllis understood the special needs of her sister and in fact often assisted her. She felt guilty about being angry with her sister for dominating the family's attention. When Phyllis's mother realized what was motivating Phyllis's behavior, she sought ways to share more exclusive attention with Phyllis.

Mother hired a specially trained babysitter, so she and Phyllis could be free to go out to lunch, to a movie or just to talk. The tantrums disappeared.

**Disruptive tantrums.** When a child's tantrum leads either to direct physical aggression (such as hitting and biting), unceasing yelling or screaming, or property destruction, then direct action is required. A two- to five-minute timeout is needed.

Tell the child sensitively but firmly, "I know how upset you are, but people are not for hitting. You need to cool off. Let me know if you want to talk." If necessary, physically remove the child.

If the child does not take you up on your offer to talk, seek him or her out after a few minutes. When you are sure he or she seems calm, say, "Looks like you're calm now. Whenever you want to leave the (timeout area) you can."

Sometime later, sit down with the child and explore the alternatives to aggression or property destruction that he or she can do when next confronted with a similar situation. This is a good time to do some planning with the child, so he or she can learn a better way to express frustration in the future.

***Out-of-control tantrums.*** Some tantrums hold the danger of injury to oneself or to another. It may sometimes be sensible to hold the child in your arms while speaking calmly and reassuringly. When kids are out of control, they feel reassured when someone takes over. As the child begins to relax, gradually release your hold while stroking and being verbally reassuring.

***Refusals.*** If a child refuses to do something important, you will need to be more persistent than she or he. Matters of health and safety fall within this category. Don't negotiate with a child who isn't heeding safety rules while riding a bike. You may well need to deny the privilege of riding until the child comes up with a plan that specifies what she or he is going to do to ensure safety.

A good night's sleep is important to health. Try putting your child's displeasure into words (you want to play some more), while setting the boundary (but it is time to brush teeth and go to sleep).

Many children react well when you give them some time to transition from one thing to the next.

—TIME FOR BED—

> While Keiko is watching TV, her mother distracts her for a moment and gains her attention. Mother says, "Right after the show, it is time to go upstairs and get ready for bed."
>
> If Mother knows that Keiko has trouble remembering or that she

needs even more help with change, then Mother reminds Keiko that there are only a few minutes left in the show and that it will soon be time to get ready for bed. The show ends, and Keiko heads up to her room.

Mother now has an opportunity to catch Keiko being good. She waits for Keiko to finish getting ready for bed. Then Mother gives Keiko a hug and offers to read her an extra bedtime story, because she was so cooperative.

When children refuse to do things which are relatively unimportant, it is best to allow natural consequences to take over. We have, for example, seen too many parents do battle with their children about wearing a winter coat (in cold climates, of course).

—BABY, IT'S COLD OUTSIDE—

Usually, the child is ready to walk out of the house on the way to school in ten degree weather with a spring jacket on, while the parent is rushing after him or her with winter coat in hand. The child says, "I don't like that coat, and I don't want to wear it."

The parent says, "You have to wear it, because it's cold outside." A power struggle has begun.

As an alternative, the parent (especially with young children) can talk about the weather, mention which coat is most appropriate to wear and even open the door briefly so the child can feel how cold it is outside before actually going out. Most kids will wear the proper attire with such an approach.

But when a child refuses, we have found that it is far better to allow the child to go outside in his or her chosen garb and directly experience the coldness. We understand that parents are concerned and might consider this a health issue. But in all the years that we have been parents and advisers to other parents, we have never seen this advice lead to a child freezing to death. A child who comes home late and misses dinner may learn much more about being on time from his or her growling stomach than from a parent lecture.

*Lying.* Most kids lie because they are afraid of trouble if they tell the truth. They usually are motivated to lie because they worry about disapproval or punishment. Our task is to make it comfortable for children to tell the truth. When we approach parenting with the attitude that a child's mistakes are the seeds by which growth and maturity develop, then we are likely to handle things in a positive way.

—HOMEWORK HASSLES—

When Dave, a fourth grader, comes home, his father asks him if he has any homework. Dave says no. A few days later Mrs. Ball, Dave's teacher, calls home to say that Dave hasn't been doing his homework. Dave's father can give Dave an angry lecture, which is certainly an understandable human response. Or he can use this as an opportunity to explore with Dave issues about school as well as honesty.

Dave's father takes the direct, I-statement approach. He says, "Dave, your teacher called today and said that your homework hasn't been getting done. I'm concerned about that, and I'd like to hear what you think."

Dave wiggles in his chair, looks away and says, "I don't know."

His father says, "You probably feel real uncomfortable now, and maybe you're even worried that what you say might get you into trouble. But the most important thing is that we figure out what's wrong in school and then how to make it better."

Dave sees that his father wants to help and starts talking.

Sometimes there is no direct evidence that a child is lying, but you have strong suspicions. When that happens, you can handle the situation by saying, "I get the feeling that I'm not getting the whole story or that the story I'm getting isn't exactly the way it happened."

If there is continued denial, be more direct without actually accusing.

Say, "I get the feeling that you're not telling me the truth about how the VCR got broken. Your honesty is very important to me, even more important than a VCR. So what else happened?"

**Sibling bickering.** There is no such thing as the always-happy family that always solves its problems thoughtfully, as depicted in "Father Knows Best" or "The Cosby Show." Problems between siblings are a good topic for family council or problem-solving meetings.

In addition, it is important to realize that most sibling bickering is really an expression of jealousy. Each child is expressing resentment at having to share Mother's or Father's attention. Each child needs special time with a parent independent of siblings.

On a daily basis, that may mean just a special hug or an arm around the shoulder for each child away from the others. On a weekly basis, that usually means having at least two ten-minute uninterrupted times of sharing in which you are available to listen fully to each child.

Another thing you can do is to appreciate and notice kids when they are playing well together. You might even want to reward them by offering a special time together. You could say, "Wow, you're getting along so well today that I want to take you both out to the movies with me."

If there are ongoing problems of rivalry, including substantial aggression, then you may want to explore a positive reward program, in which the kids earn specific rewards for not fighting. Finally, you could use a timeout, during which the children are separated from each other for a few minutes. Tell them to think about a plan to stop the bickering.

When children blame each other, redirect their attention onto themselves. Ask, "I hear that he started it, but what did you do?" Persist in using the broken record until each child acknowledges how he or she contributed to the problem and what she or he will do to stop.

**Sharing.** Most parents stare in horror as their sweet little child grabs from other children and refuses to share. In fact, children really aren't ready to begin sharing until sometime between ages three and four.

To encourage sharing, wait until you see your child actually sharing something, either with you or a friend, and notice it in a positive way. You could say, with an arm around her shoulder, "Jill, you really tried to make Gail happy by sharing your doll with her. That was very special."

Let children see you volunteering your time to share with others. Have them assist you in putting together a package of clothes to donate. Ask them which of their things they'd like to donate to people in need. Support, encourage and reinforce their efforts at sharing when they do get involved.

***Mealtimes.*** There are perhaps more battles fought at the table between parents and children than anywhere else. Most children go through a period—ranging from a few months to the rest of their lives—when they don't want to eat what Mother or Father has prepared.

My 13 year old lived for several years on peanut butter and jelly. Only gradually did he expand his food preferences. Even now, he is fussy about what he'll eat.

This problem begins when a parent prepares a meal and a child objects to its contents. The parent has usually spent some time preparing the food and feels angry at the child's rejection.

—ONE MOTHER'S STORY—

> The mother of a nine-year-old child told the following story when she brought the girl in for counseling because of defiance:
>
> We constantly fight during meals. She either whines, won't eat, criticizes the meal or dawdles. I just want to pull her hair out sometimes. Then last week, we all sat down to eat a meal, and she brought a box to the table, setting it down beside her. When I asked why the box was there, she said that it was for food that she was going to donate from her plate to the starving children of Ethiopia!

There are several effective things to do during mealtimes. First of all, it is absolutely normal for most children to develop specific taste preferences for foods and to want to eat only that which they like. If what they want provides proper nourishment, you can avoid many power struggles by simply allowing children to eat what they like.

To avoid preparing several meals to accommodate all tastes, you can tell children they are free to prepare a different meal if they don't like the one put in front of them. (Keep a jar of peanut butter handy.)

If the child just likes to complain, we've found that having a two-complaint-per-meal rule makes sense. Each child is allowed two negatives such as "Ugh, I hate this" per meal. When the third complaint is heard, the kids know that the meal will be removed with no in-between snacks allowed until the next meal.

If the meal is removed, it should be done matter-of-factly. "Thomas, that's your third complaint. I guess you're not very hungry tonight," says Mom, as she removes his meal.

When the problem is dawdling, you want to be sure that the child hasn't affected his or her appetite by snacking in between meals. During mealtime, serve the food, including at least one of his or her favorites. Then let the child eat at his or her own pace.

Realize that young children will often either eat too fast (they have many better things to do) or too slow (they are still mastering skills such as using a fork, cutting food, etc.). When the family has finished the meal, and it is clear that the child is indeed dawdling, say politely, "The meal is over," as you begin to clear the table. If the child protests that she or he hasn't finished, tell her or him in a dignified way, "Too bad there wasn't enough time to finish, but this meal is over."

*Saying no.* What you do when a child says no to some or all of your requests depends on the age of the child. At some ages, saying no is both normal and necessary. Children begin to develop their own sense of identity by saying no to parents; they establish themselves as separate and independent from parents.

This is important to do. Were children always to say yes, they would be little more than extensions of their parents. Peak ages for saying no during

Common Problems, Situations and Solutions _____ 113

early childhood are 18 months (this is one of the toddler's first words), two and one-half years, and four years.

Don't ask yes or no questions. You can count on the fact that during these ages any time you ask a question such as Do you want...? or Would you like...? the answer will always be no, unless the question has to do with a brand-new bike or some other desirable item.

Provide simple but real choices. For example: You can hang up your coat on this hook or on that hook. You can have peanut butter or grilled cheese for lunch.

Decide on specific consequences for each no. A no to eating can be simply dealt with by allowing the natural consequence of hunger to affect the child's stomach. For this to be effective, you must be sure that there are no in-between snacks.

A no to putting toys away can result in loss of the toy for a brief time or putting all of the toys lying around into an out-of-the-way box, from which they can be reclaimed only on a certain day. If left unclaimed, these toys can be donated to a charitable organization.

—SLEEPING CARS—

A method I used with success was to tell my six-year-old son that any toys left lying around would be put in his bed, because of the danger that others might trip on the toys if they were left out. For a few weeks, there were no visible results. (He wasn't getting any better at putting toys away.)

But one night he went to bed somewhere in that dreamy state between awake and asleep, and he plopped down on his bed right smack in the middle of Matchbox cars, books and other goodies. The mild but certain discomfort to his back caused by metal rather than mattress resulted in at least a temporary cure.

A last strategy offered when saying no is a major problem is to consider a positive reward program.

One final word: you want to get results, so don't concern yourself with the child's words. If the child says no but does what you want, then he or she is probably just going through a very temporary developmental phase. As a caring adult, you can always acknowledge a child's feelings, no matter how different they are from yours, while at the same time holding firm to important expectations and demands that grow from your wisdom.

*Swearing.* My five year old came home from school one day and held his middle finger in the air as he asked, "What does this mean?" About a year earlier, we had had a lengthy discussion about using the *f-word*. He had come home with this knowledge from preschool and decided to use the word many times in different situations at home.

At first, I ignored it and hoped that it would simply disappear (which it did not). So I explained that the word bothered a lot of people, because it was an especially nasty way of saying I hate you.

I told him that using that word at home was unacceptable. If he really had to say it, then the best thing to do would be to go to his room, put a pillow over his face and say the word into the pillow so that nobody else would be upset.

Two things happened: he said it much less, and he did a few times use the pillow, probably because this was a new and different thing for him to do. Later, when he asked about the raised finger, I only had to tell him that it meant the same as the *f-word*.

It is rarely necessary to do much more than this. Kids need to know what words mean, how their behavior makes other people feel, why rules exist and other, more acceptable ways to say the same thing. Swearing usually starts during the later preschool years. The kind of explanation offered above combined with ignoring the swearing is usually all that is needed.

*Stealing.* When your child comes home with something that you know does not belong to him or her, ask where it came from. If the child makes up a story that you know stretches any possible reality, then confront him or her by saying simply I don't believe you. You follow this up by asking again. Let the child know that telling the truth is important to do and that no matter where the item came from, it is a problem that can be solved.

When you are told the details, you should go to wherever the incident occurred with your child and see to it that he or she returns the item. If you cannot find out where the item came from, then simply say, "I am upset that you are not telling me where you got these things, but I know these aren't yours so I'll need to keep them." Discard these items later.

When stealing is a recurrent problem, it is usually a signal that a child is feeling deprived of material goods, affection or both. In our work with teachers, we have found it helpful for teachers to give things to children who steal. Often such children really want to keep part of the class with them at all times.

Therefore, if you know that a child has taken another child's crayons, you can see that the first child gets the crayons back, while the second child, at some later time (not right after the stealing, because that might wrongly signal that you approve of stealing), is given a few crayons, papers or even a picture of the teacher to take home. Teachers who have done this have reported that there are often dramatic decreases in the amount of things missing from the classroom.

**Babysitter or daycare authority.** Some children will be perfect angels in the presence of their parents but quite the opposite while at daycare or with the babysitter. Several factors contribute to this problem. First of all, many parents feel guilty at leaving their children, even if they have no other choice. Because of their guilt, they may think that every minute they spend with their child must be positive, giving and nondisciplinary.

Parents must realize that discipline is an important and necessary part of their job. Children need to experience first-hand the direct consequences or appreciations from parents regarding their behavior. It is rarely, if ever, good practice to give in to your guilt. Kids who have learned that their parents will always give-me-now are unprepared to handle the realities present in the best of daycare settings.

When children leave the house armed with a solid foundation of respect for the rights of others, as well as the message that you can't always have what you want this instant, they are much better able to extend those values in many situations.

Secondly, whom you choose for daycare is an extremely important decision that cannot be taken lightly. You need to select a person or agency with values that are consistent with your own. You should observe the caregivers in action.

How do they deal with conflict between children? What kinds of attention are available to the children in this situation? When children break rules, what is done for discipline? Once you choose, you need to make it clear to your child that the caregiver is in charge and that you expect the child to behave properly in that situation.

Finally, you should be clear and specific with the caregiver about methods of offering attention and discipline that tend to be most effective with your child. Leaving a child to the care of others is never an easy decision, but following these guidelines can help make the experience rewarding for your child.

*A new baby.* It is our experience that the birth of a new baby is always a major event in a family. It generates feelings of excitement as well as dread. No matter how well you prepare your children for the arrival of a baby, the reality will almost always throw their lives (and yours) into disarray.

They will get less of your attention. There will be a cute but loud baby crying during their favorite TV show. They will at least some of the time be inconvenienced to get a diaper or hold the baby. In some situations, they will be expected to play a major role in the daily upbringing of the child.

Reassure your older children that feelings of resentment, annoyance and anger toward the new baby are understandable and normal. You might even share that even though you love this baby, you sometimes resent your loss of freedom.

Assign small but manageable responsibilities for the baby's care to older children. Be sure to appreciate older children as they hold the baby, change diapers, play with the baby or if old enough, even babysit. Children should not be given babysitting responsibilities for an infant until at least the age of 13.

We have seen too many children as young as five and six be given major responsibilities for the care of their younger siblings. A six year old cannot correctly manage an infant, much less a two year old. A nine year old should not be asked to watch any child under six for longer than a few minutes.

Ask children to assume only those responsibilities with which they can be successful. To do otherwise is to risk your older child's self-esteem (kids feel bad when their parents ask them to do something and they don't succeed) and your younger children's safety.

Teachers can provide an opportunity for children to share their ambivalent feelings about having a new baby or being burdened with responsibilities that may feel overwhelming. Ask children to write a story about how they feel about a new baby brother or sister.

Offer a little extra love and support, as many children feel insecure about their place in the family. Reassure them that you are available to listen to their feelings, concerns and joys about this important change in their lives.

# Recurrent Problems

One principle of human behavior is that we keep doing things that are followed by positive consequences, good feelings or rewards, and we stop doing things that are followed by negative consequences, bad feelings or no rewards.

People learn to behave according to the consequences of their behavior. *Reinforcers* are positive consequences of behavior that encourage those behaviors. Sometimes special reinforcers are purposely used to reward good behavior.

Let's examine when, how and with whom to use a systematic program of reinforcement. But first, let's look at the different types of rewards or reinforcers.

When your supervisor tells you that you did a good job while he or she pats you on the back, he or she is reinforcing your behavior. He or she knows that all people want to be noticed in positive ways and that such notice might well increase your productivity on the job. That is a type of *social reinforcer.*

In order for the pat on the back to be felt by you as a reward, you must believe it was genuinely given and view the giver as a person from whom you want reinforcement. Otherwise, the reward will mean little and is unlikely to influence your future behavior.

Getting a bonus at the end of the year or after a job well done is another type of reinforcer—*concrete reinforcer.* Concrete reinforcers are tangible—money, toys, clothes, food.

An *activity reinforcer* means doing something pleasant and desirable after a less desirable task or job is done. Looking forward to a movie after cleaning the house is a way to reward yourself with a preferred activity after successfully completing a less preferred one. Eating dessert after vegetables is another example.

A final type of reinforcer is *token reinforcer.* These are poker chips, points, stickers or stars that can be exchanged for desirable things. Technically, money is a token reinforcer, because by itself, it is meaningless. Money has reinforcement value only because it will purchase other desirable things.

All children need to be noticed and appreciated by others important in their lives. That is a basic human need. Most children do not need a systematic, formal program of reinforcement, because they naturally get enough reinforcement from parents and others in their environment to behave effectively.

However, some children either cannot or will not control their behavior. They become disruptive to others, damage property and are unable to perform in most situations as well as they otherwise might. Some of these children have had inconsistent or inadequate parenting, while others may have challenging temperaments.

Children with such labels as behaviorally disturbed, learning disabled, attention deficit or hyperactivity disorder, et al., often have difficulty with self-control. This difficulty may warrant involvement with a specific reinforcement program.

Reinforcement programs can also be implemented by parents or teachers who are dealing with specific but recurrent problems such as fighting, being late to school, coming home late, keeping a messy room, not doing homework or household chores. Before starting a reinforcement program for these behaviors, we would advise you to first send I-statements expressing your concern to the child. Work with the child to develop a plan for better future behavior. Then meet with the child (if need be, several times) to see if together you can problem-solve a good solution. Before instituting a formal reinforcement program, explore the many other methods, ideas and strategies in this book.

The leading concept that drives reinforcement programs is to catch kids when they are good. While that may sound simple, it is often hard to remember to do. In schools, the ratio of negative to positive comments used by teachers when they talk with kids is approximately ten-to-one.

That means that for every positive comment made, there are ten negatives. That type of ratio seems to be true for parents as well. Consider the frequency at the supermarket with which parents criticize or yell versus appreciate or reinforce.

Rarely will we remind ourselves to tell Ray, who too often hits, that he is really playing well today after a half hour of no fighting. We are much more likely to notice Ray when he is fighting. Ray and all children learn to continue doing the things that are reinforced. (e.g., If I can get attention for negative behavior, then I'll keep doing that. Irritating and annoying others can be a powerful way for me to get attention.)

There have to be concrete incentives for some children to make better choices. Children need to learn that behaving in appropriate, socially acceptable ways leads to at least as much reinforcement as continuing in their old ways. Let's look at the elements of a reinforcement program.

***Take small steps.*** Behavior changes slowly and gradually. If a child is frequently aggressive or forgetful, rarely sits still or follows directions, her or his behavior probably will not change quickly. There is nothing you can do to make behavior change occur more rapidly. To expect that is like expecting an infant to walk before she or he crawls.

—No Way—

> Jesse was a fourth grader who was frequently in trouble at school. He often received poor grades, and phone calls from school to home were common. His teacher and parents agreed that he would lose 15 minutes of TV time each night that he received a negative report from school.
>
> After a few weeks, there was little change. When Jesse was asked why he wasn't doing better, he said simply, "It doesn't matter what I do. I could be having a great day and then one little thing goes wrong and that's it! There's just no way I can be perfect like they want."

In this case, the teacher and parents probably could have gotten better results if the program enabled Jesse to earn rather than lose privileges and specific standards for success were specified.

We must learn to reinforce small changes. At first you may need to reward your child every half hour (or less) when he or she hasn't hit his or her younger brother or sister.

***Chart the behavior.*** A reinforcing program is usually used when children are misbehaving often, so it is important to know how often the behavior is occurring before we do anything differently. Then we can compare behavior before and after the program. In that way, we can know whether the program is effective.

If we know that Samantha hits her brother an average of eight times per day before we start a reinforcing program, we can use that figure as a basis of comparison to see if she hits her brother less frequently after the program has begun. It is therefore important to chart the specific behavior that you want to change (see Figure 1). Then both you and the child will be able to see successful change when it happens.

**Establish a standard for success.** Once you know the extent of the problem, it is then necessary to define success. If Samantha hits her

FIGURE 1
## Charting a Problem Behavior

1. What is the behavior you are charting? Be sure to describe it in clear, specific terms. You have to be able to see or hear the behavior.

Behavior:


2. Fill in the chart below for at least one week before you actually start a reinforcement program.

| DAY | How often did the behavior occur today? (Put a mark next to the day each time the behavior occurs.) | Action(s) You Took |
|---|---|---|
| Monday | | |
| Tuesday | | |
| Wednesday | | |
| Thursday | | |
| Friday | | |
| Saturday | | |
| Sunday | | |

*Am I in Trouble?*

brother four times a day instead of eight, is that success? Should she be rewarded? Might Samantha still conclude that hitting is OK as long as it occurs less often?

In order to resolve these questions, we think it best to establish positive goals, rather than less negative ones. Usually, a 25 percent to 50 percent reduction in the problem behavior is a good goal. It's even better to figure out the reverse of the problem behavior (e.g., messy/tidy room, hitting/telling when angry, arguing/playing cooperatively). Then give rewards when the good behavior occurs.

—SAMANTHA'S PLAN—

First, Samantha needs to know what she can do that is more acceptable than hitting. When she feels frustrated or simply wants to have her way, she can walk away, tell her brother she is angry, take charge by telling him that it is her turn next, or tell Mom. Samantha can practice doing each of these things. She can develop a plan to do one or more of these things.

Now we are ready for a reinforcing plan. Samantha is told that for each hour on weekdays that she and her brother are able to get along without fighting, she will earn a point. Mom tells Samantha that when she has earned five points daily for two days in a row, she will earn a reward. Her reward could be a special trip with Mom to the local ice-cream parlor. Mother and Samantha keep a chart of Samantha's points (see Figure 2). A special weekend chart could also be developed.

As Samantha meets these goals, the criteria for earning a reward increase. Eventually, rewards are stopped because she shows lots of good grown-up behavior and can be treated like a big girl.

Whatever the standards, there should be a 90 percent chance that the child will be successful from the beginning in order to establish a positive momentum. You must remember to make success reachable.

## FIGURE 2
## Point Chart

| DAY | Before School | | After School | | | | | Total | Reward Earned Yes /No |
|---|---|---|---|---|---|---|---|---|---|
| | 7-8 AM | 8-9 AM | 3-4 PM | 4-5 PM | 5-6 PM | 6-7 PM | 7-8 PM | | |
| Monday | X | X | X | O | X | X | O | 5 | No |
| Tuesday | X | X | O | O | X | X | X | 5 | Yes |
| Wednesday | X | O | O | O | X | X | O | 3 | No |
| Thursday | X | X | X | O | X | X | X | 6 | No |
| Friday | X | X | X | O | X | X | O | 5 | Yes |

X = Samantha earns a point for getting along with brother

O = Samantha does not earn a point

***Identify reinforcers.*** Decide what is rewarding or reinforcing to the child. List things like food preferences, places and people to visit, enjoyable activities and desirable things. Figure out which of these are big things (worth many points) and which are small things (worth one or a few points). Ideally, a program should contain some of each type of reward. Then you and the child can decide which rewards he or she will work for.

Samantha's mother knows that ice cream is pleasurable. It is reinforcing. Of course, if Samantha were allergic to ice cream and broke out in hives each time she ate it, it wouldn't be an effective reinforcer. Identifying reinforcers that will be effective for the child is an important key to success.

The idea is that children earn what they like by behaving in acceptable ways. Think about all the things the child seems to enjoy (activities, items, positive comments or attention). Make a list of these. Specify to the child what he or she needs to do to earn one or more of the things on the list. You can even make the child a partner in the program by asking, "What would you like to earn after...?"

***Give the reinforcement.*** Generally, it is best to give the reward as soon after the occurrence of the positive behavior as possible.

—REWARDING WORDS—

> Billy, you really put in time cleaning your room (behavior). Thanks so much for the cooperation. That means a lot to me.

> Samantha, I noticed that when you got upset, you told your brother you were angry and you didn't hit (behavior). Way to go! (verbal reinforcer). You also earned a point toward that ice cream (with a big nourishing smile).

A chart will help you and the child see how she or he is doing. It will show when or whether a reward has been earned. Resist any and all efforts the child might make to get the reward if it has not been earned.

One of the principles of successful reinforcement is to reinforce every right response early on while the child is learning the good habit. Then later, to keep him or her following these habits, reinforce occasionally.

In other words, in the early going, you will reinforce every single one of Billy's clean-up behaviors. Every time you see him put something away, you'll express your pleasure and maybe offer him a small, special treat. But after this desirable behavior has become automatic, you will need to only occasionally do the same.

—I'M PROUD OF YOU—

> It is best to say something such as "Billy, what you just did is big-boy, grown-up behavior. Can you tell me what it is?" If Billy can't tell you, say, "Putting things away without having to be reminded is grown-up. Gosh, Billy, I am proud of you."

Common Problems, Situations and Solutions _____ 125

***Use timeout.*** Suppose Samantha loses her cool and hits her brother. One thing that can be effective is to give Samantha a few minutes of timeout, so she can calm down and think things over.

—SAMANTHA'S TIMEOUT—

Mom says firmly, "Samantha, people are not for hitting. I'm disappointed. Take a five-minute timeout. Then tell me what you could have done instead to earn a point."

After the five minutes, Samantha says she could have walked away or told Mom. Mom hugs her and wishes her good luck in doing one of these things the next time she feels like hitting. (With younger children who haven't yet developed a concept of time, setting a kitchen timer is a good alternative.)

***Turn responsibility for the program over to the child.*** The eventual goal of reinforcement programs is that children will learn to reward themselves after a period of success. If we keep rewarding children with things like candy, stickers, etc., they will eventually become dependent on and perhaps even addicted to the reward.

Gradually turn over the responsibility for rewards to the child. When the child has done well for several weeks, suggest that he or she now seems sufficiently mature and grown up to handle these big boy or girl responsibilities by him- or herself, without needing a reward. Be sure the child gets plenty of attention when he or she is doing things correctly and behaving responsibly.

Just the other day, I was testing an alert, capable three-year-old child who asked every 30 seconds if she could have a sticker. At an early age, she has become hooked on rewards. Without them, she does not perform. We want to use rewards only temporarily and only until children develop a good habit.

Rewards can also be abused. The mother of a sixth grader recently came to me because her extremely bright son absolutely refused to do any homework. His grades were suffering.

A few months earlier, this mother had promised her son that if he brought home better grades, he could earn a trip to Florida. For two months, the boy did much better at his work. He then went on the trip. When the trip ended, so did his effort.

Expensive rewards can backfire. They falsely lead children to conclude that they can have excessive rewards for behaving in a responsible way.

In most instances, we consider rewards as a stopgap measure that helps the child exercise self-control. Once the child begins to develop self-control, we want to shift the focus to the child's sense of pride in becoming more responsible. Teaching children responsibility is the ultimate goal of discipline.

# Conclusion

Raising children is perhaps the single most difficult endeavor modern people undertake. Even the experts deal with confusion, unanswered questions, serious problems and doubts while raising children.

It is easier to do almost anything else than it is to be a parent. Writers and thinkers from Mr. Spock to Dr. Spock have offered millions of strategies, suggestions, guidelines and hints. Still, parents wonder daily if they are doing the right thing.

As our children get older, our parenting skills and our understanding increase, but the problems become more perplexing. Eventually, crying for milk evolves into demanding money for video games.

Our mothers and fathers tell us that the old-fashioned way was better than the way we are doing it, just as our grandparents told them. We notice other parents, some who seem to have everything under control and some who make us wonder why tests aren't required before parenting is allowed.

We hope that the activities, methods and principles for responsibility offered in this book will clarify the issues and offer you a framework for decision making about discipline. We offer our ideas with humility. Between us, we have six children, and there have been many times when we wished theories worked as well in the home as they do in books.

Years ago, one of my children pulled one of our earlier books on classroom discipline off the shelf. "You said on page 65 not to yell," he angrily shouted, "and yet you are yelling at me. If you don't stop, I'll call your publisher and tell him what you're really like." The child was only eight years old at the time.

Remember that reading about parenting is easier than doing it. However, doing it is one of life's great treasures. That eight-year-old child who threatened to call the publisher gave his dad an unsolicited backrub the very same day, saying, "You're having a bad day, too. Maybe this will help."

# References

Armstrong, T. 1987. *In their own way.* Los Angeles: Jeremy Tarcher.

Curwin, R. and Mendler, A. 1988. *Discipline with dignity.* Reston, VA: Association for Supervision and Curriculum Development.

Curwin, R. and Mendler, A. 1980. *The discipline book: A complete guide to school and classroom management.* Reston, VA: Reston Publishing Co.

Dinkmeyer, D. and McKay, G.P. 1982. *Systematic training for effective parenting: The parents' guide.* Circle Pines, MN: American Guidance.

Driekurs, R. 1964. *Children: The challenge.* New York: Hawthorn Books. Rudolph Driekurs and Donald Dinkmeyer are the two best sources on natural consequences with children.

Driekurs, R. and Cassel, P. 1972. *Discipline without tears: What to do with children who misbehave.* New York: Hawthorn Books.

Elkind, D. 1981. *The hurried child.* Reading, MA: Addison Wesley Publishing Co.

Faber, A. and Mazlish, E. 1982. *How to talk so kids will listen and listen so kids will talk.* New York: Avon Books.

Glasser, W. 1984. *Control theory: A new explanation of how we control our lives.* New York: Harper and Row.

Ilg, F. L. and Ames, L. B. 1972. *Child behavior from birth to ten.* New York: Barnes and Noble.

Mendler, A. 1990. *Smiling at yourself: Educating young children about stress and self-esteem.* Santa Cruz, CA: Network Publications.

Mendler, A. and Curwin, R. 1983. *Taking charge in the classroom.* Reston, VA: Reston Publishing Co.

Schmitt, B. D. 1987. *Your child's health.* New York: Bantam Books.

Seligman, M. E. P. 1981. A learned helplessness point of view. In *Behavior therapy for depression.* New York: Academic Press.

Selye, H. 1974. *Stress without distress.* New York: The New American Library.

Slavin, R. 1983. *Cooperative learning.* New York: Longman.

Stock, G. 1988. *The kids' book of questions.* New York: Workman Publishing.

Tournier, P. 1989. To resist or surrender. In *Raising positive kids in a negative world,* ed. Z. Ziglar. New York: Ballantine Books.

Wlodkowski, R. and Jaynes, J. 1990. *Eager to learn.* San Francisco: Jossey Bass.